Contents

© School Zone Publishing Company

What's in This Book

Sit back, buckle your seat belt, and get ready for a state-by-state tour of the United States of America. Visit our neighbors to the north and south, too.

In this activity book, you'll pick up some interesting facts about the states to amaze your friends and family. You'll practice reading maps that show some of the cities, highways, national parks, and other features you can find in the states. On top of that, you'll enjoy some of your favorite kinds of puzzles: crosswords, dot-to-dots, mazes, and plenty of others.

On pages 58 and 59, you'll find an outline map of the United States. After you finish the activities for each state, you can turn to this map, color in the state, and write its name.

Northwest Poir
Military Area

1
City West

Harborto

Southern
Island

North National Park
25
Northpoint
Northwest Bay
Bay Town
Westward River
25
Upper Lake
Indian Reservation
1
Weston
Central
Lower Lake
25
Lookout Mountains
Southside
ational Park
Southport Ocean

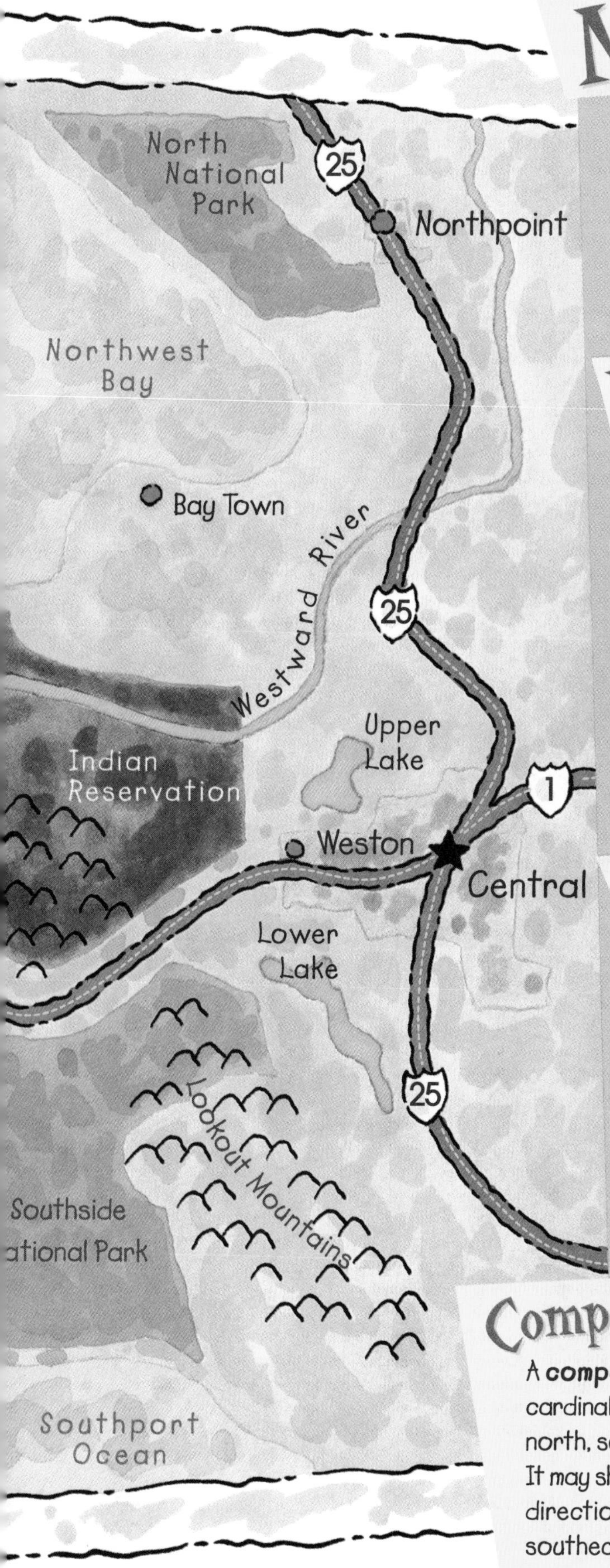

Map Basics

A **map** is a picture of a place. Maps can show land, water, highways, mountains, and many other things.

Notice that the sizes of the names of cities and towns vary. The larger the city, the larger its name appears on the map. On this map **Central** is bigger than **Northpoint**. **Northpoint** is bigger than **Bay Town**.

Legend

A **legend** or **key** is a box that contains symbols used on a map. The legend explains what those symbols mean. Here are some of the symbols you will find in this book.

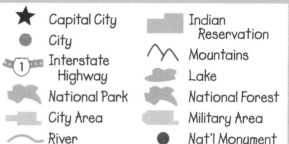

Capital City
City
1
Interstate Highway
National Park
City Area
River
Indian Reservation
Mountains
Lake
National Forest
Military Area
Nat'l Monument

Scale

A map can show a town, a state, a country, or the whole world. How can you tell the distances shown on a map? You use a **map scale**. Here's one.

miles
0 10 20 30 40 50 60 70 80 90 100
0 20 40 60 80 100 120 140 160
kilometers

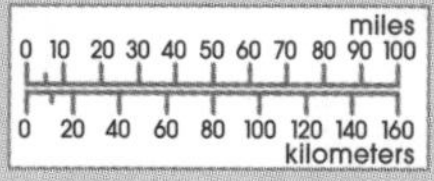

On this scale, one inch equals 100 miles, or 160 kilometers. If a city on the map is 1/2 inch from another city, it is 50 miles, or 80 kilometers, away. If one city is 2 inches from another, it is ________ miles away.

Compass Rose

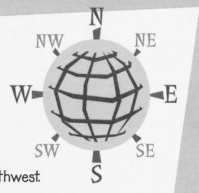

A **compass rose** shows the cardinal directions on a map: north, south, east, and west. It may show the in-between directions, too: northeast, southeast, southwest, and northwest.

N
NW
NE
W
E
SW
SE
S

Alabama

The Heart of Dixie

Yellowhammer

Camellia

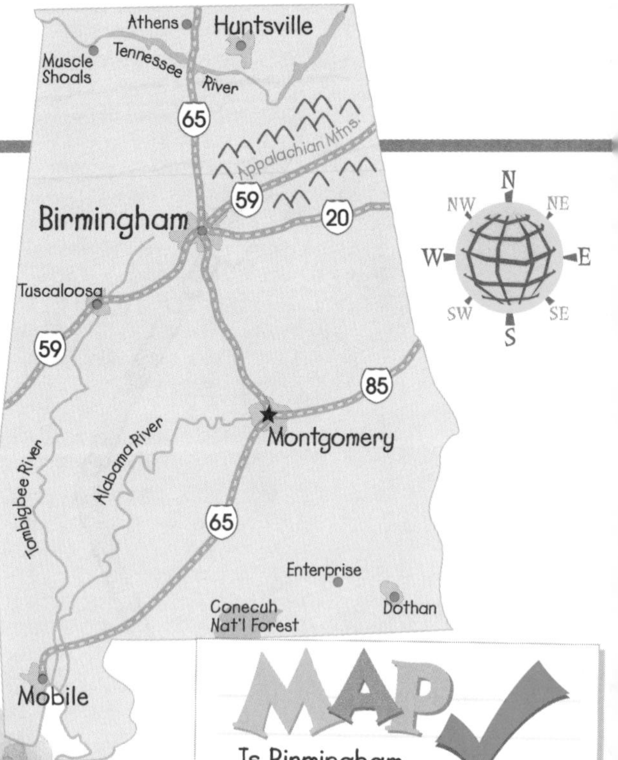

Athens
Huntsville
Muscle Shoals
Tennessee River
65
Appalachian Mts.
59
20
Birmingham
Tuscaloosa
59
85
Tombigbee River
Alabama River
Montgomery
65
Enterprise
Conecuh Nat'l Forest
Dothan
Mobile
N
NE
E
SE
S
SW
W
NW

Trolley Tracks

The first electric trolley cars in the U.S. began operating in Montgomery in 1866. These three trolleys are headed back to the trolley barn. Which has the shortest distance to go?

TROLLEY BARN

MAP ✓

Is Birmingham north or south of the capital, Montgomery?

FOR REAL!

In 1919, the town of Enterprise put up an unusual monument of thanks—a statue of a cotton-eating insect, the boll weevil. After the pesky insect ate all their cotton, farmers in Enterprise grew lots of different crops and became richer than before.

Alaska

The Last Frontier

Willow Ptarmigan

Forget-Me-Not

Barrow

Beaufort Sea

Brooks Range

TransAlaska Pipeline

Gates of the Arctic Nat'l Park

Kotzebue Sound

Kotzebue

Nome

Norton Sound

Yukon River

Fairbanks

Mount McKinley

Denali Nat'l Park

Alaska Highway

Anchorage

Yukon River

Akolmiut

Alaska Range

Bethel

Seward

Gulf of Alaska

Juneau

Petersburg

Sitka

Ketchikan

Kodiak

Bristol Bay

Aleutian Islands

Legend
★ Capital City
● City
Alaska Highway
National Park
City Area
River
Mountains
Pipeline
National Forest

MAP ✓
Which city is bigger: Barrow or Bethel?

Hidden Resources

Alaska has more than any other state. More what?
Cross off the **v**s, **x**s, **y**s, and **z**s to find out.

x x i v v y x n x x y v v l x x v

z z a v x y n x v d y w y z z z

v a x y t v z z y e v z r z z

_____

-FOR- REAL!

Temperatures in Alaska can drop as low as –80 °F and go as high as 100 °F. That's quite a range! Better pack your mittens AND your swimsuit!

Arizona

The Grand Canyon State

Cactus Wren

Saguaro Cactus

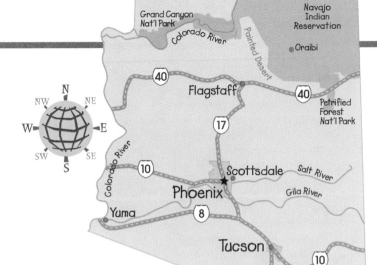

Nature Search

Visitors enjoy Arizona's amazing and beautiful scenic places, including the Grand Canyon, Painted Desert, and Petrified Forest. Here are some names of natural features, plants, and animals of Arizona. How many can you find in the puzzle?

MAP ✓

Which interstate highway goes through Flagstaff?

BUTTE	HILL
CANYON	MESA
PINNACLE	CHOLLA
VALLEY	YUCCA
TERRACE	DEER
SAGUARO	ELK
ANTELOPE	BEAR
BOBCAT	

A	K	S	A	K	B	C	R	O
C	B	S	A	G	U	A	R	O
P	E	O	S	A	T	N	T	K
I	A	N	B	L	T	Y	Y	D
N	R	P	I	C	E	O	L	E
N	C	K	E	S	A	N	L	E
A	Y	H	C	V	I	T	O	R
C	R	P	O	A	M	E	S	A
L	M	Y	N	L	T	R	U	P
E	P	E	L	L	L	R	K	M
Y	C	L	S	E	Y	A	S	L
C	I	K	N	Y	U	C	C	A
H	S	P	B	K	I	E	L	H
B	A	N	T	E	L	O	P	E

-FOR- REAL!

Oraibi may be the oldest town in the U.S. Hopi Indians built the settlement over 800 years ago, and people have lived there ever since.

Arkansas

The Natural State

Mockingbird

Apple Blossom

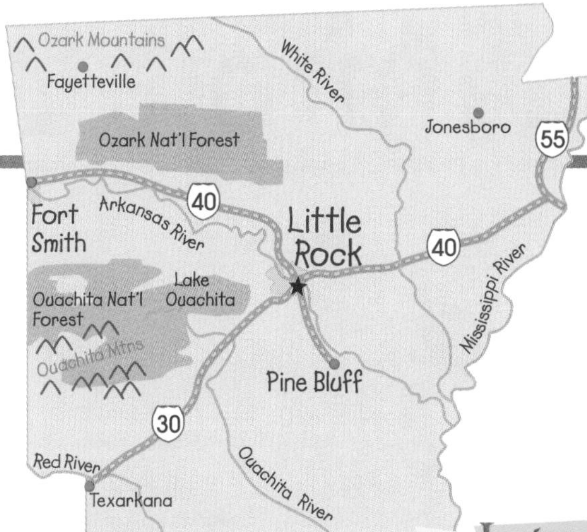

Ozark Mountains
Fayetteville
White River
Jonesboro
55
Ozark Nat'l Forest
40
Fort Smith
Arkansas River
Little Rock
40
Mississippi River
Lake Ouachita
Ouachita Nat'l Forest
Ouachita Mtns
Pine Bluff
30
Red River
Texarkana
Ouachita River

Legend

- ★ Capital City
- City
- Interstate Highway
- National Park
- City Area
- River
- Mountains
- Indian Reservation
- National Forest
- Lake

MAP ✓

What river borders Arkansas on the east?

Carat Hunt

Arkansas has the only working diamond mine in the United States. Visitors can keep the diamonds they find! How many diamonds can you find in this picture?

OH! A DIAMOND IN THE ROUGH!
Post Office

-FOR- REAL!

The city of Texarkana is divided down the middle between Arkansas and Texas. It has two governments and a post office building that stands in both states.

California

CALIFORNIA REPUBLIC

The Golden State

California Valley Quail

Golden Poppy

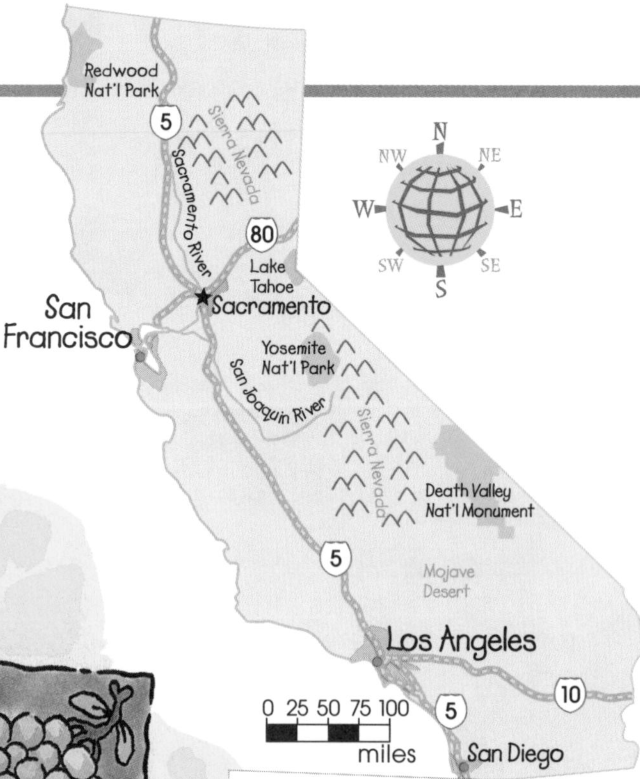

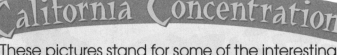

Redwood Nat'l Park
5
Sierra Nevada
Sacramento River
80
Lake Tahoe
Sacramento
San Francisco
Yosemite Nat'l Park
San Joaquin River
Sierra Nevada
Death Valley Nat'l Monument
5
Mojave Desert
Los Angeles
10
0 25 50 75 100
miles
5
San Diego
N
NE
E
SE
S
SW
W
NW

California Concentration

These pictures stand for some of the interesting things to see and places to go in California. Play a memory game. Study the pictures for about 30 seconds. Then close the book. How many things can you remember?

HOLLYWOOD

MAP ✓

Which cities are closer, San Francisco and Sacramento or Los Angeles and San Diego?

-FOR- REAL! California's coast redwood trees are the tallest living things in the world.

Colorado

The Centennial State

Lark Bunting

Rocky Mountain Columbine

Fort Collins — 25
Greeley — 76
Boulder
70 — Denver
Colorado River
Aspen
Grand Junction
Pikes Peak elv. 14,110 ft
70
Colorado Springs
Pueblo
Royal Gorge
Arkansas River
Rio Grande River — 25

Mountains

0 20 40 60 80 100
miles

Legend
★ Capital City
● City
20 Interstate Highway
National Park
City Area
River
Mountains
Lake

Capital Code

Do you know the nickname of Colorado's capital, Denver? Start at the ▼. Write every third letter to find out.

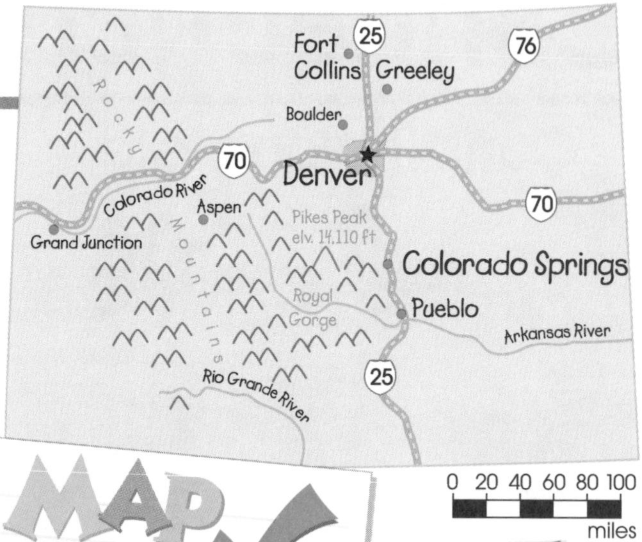

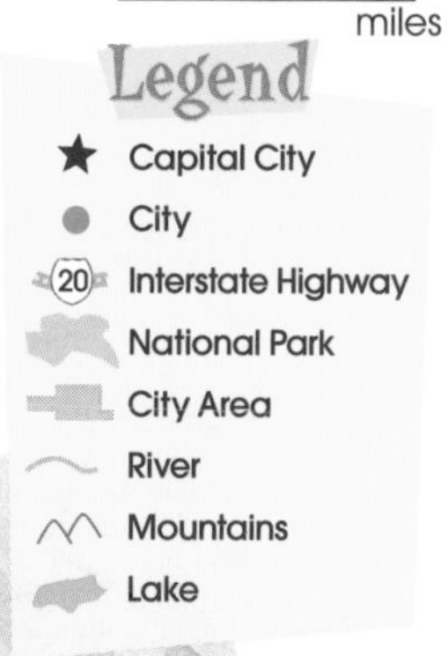

MAP ✔

Which cities on the map are within 100 miles of Denver?

STNWYCZMBXIVWLDREGNHSBITYGNKHPACUMIJ

_____

FOR REAL!

The Colorado River, which flows through canyons of red rock, got its name from the Spanish word **colorado**, or "colored red." The state was named for the river.

Connecticut

The Constitution State

Robin

Mountain Laurel

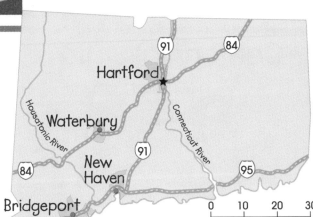

Hartford • 91 • 84
Housatonic River
Waterbury
91
Connecticut River
New Haven
84
95
Bridgeport
Stamford • 95

0 10 20 30
miles

N
NW NE
W E
SW SE
S

Find the Firsts!

Connecticut is the home of many historical firsts. Follow the maze to find out what some of them are. Watch out! You won't be able to find a path to the inventions that are **not** Connecticut firsts!

MAP ✓

Measure one of the state's highways. How many inches long is it? How many miles does that represent?

DOT DOT DOT DIT DOT DIT DIT DIT DOT
1837 - THE FIRST TELEGRAPH

1954 - THE FIRST NUCLEAR-POWERED SUBMARINE

1864 - THE FIRST INSURANCE POLICY

1790 - THE FIRST SPINNING MACHINES

1878 - THE FIRST TELEPHONE EXCHANGE

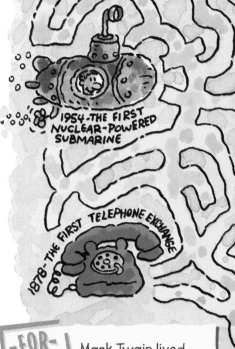

1884 - THE FIRST SKYSCRAPER

1889 - THE FIRST FOOTBALL TACKLING DUMMY

1796 - THE FIRST COOKBOOK

-FOR-REAL! Mark Twain lived in Hartford in the late 1800s. You can still visit his house today.

Delaware

DECEMBER 7, 1787

he First State

Blue Hen Chicken

Peach Blossom

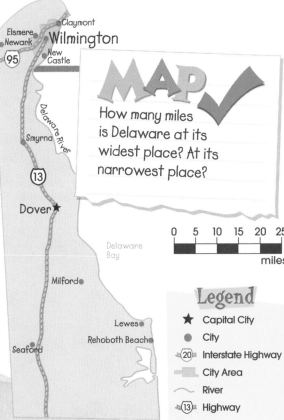

Claymont
Elsmere • Newark • Wilmington
95
New Castle

Delaware River

Smyrna •

13

Dover ★

Delaware Bay

Milford •

Lewes •
Rehoboth Beach •

Seaford •

MAP ✓

How many miles is Delaware at its widest place? At its narrowest place?

0 5 10 15 20 25

miles

Legend
★ Capital City
● City
20 Interstate Highway
City Area
River
13 Highway

Catch the Cluckers

Broiler chickens, chickens 5 to 12 weeks old, are Delaware's most important farm product. Look at the barnyard. How many chickens can you find?

-FOR- REAL! Chemists at the DuPont Company combined water, air, and coal by-products to produce nylon, a lightweight fabric that didn't wrinkle. The new fabric came on the market in 1938.

Florida

The Sunshine State

Mockingbird

Orange Blossom

MAP ✓
Is the capital of Florida also the largest city? How can you tell?

Pensacola • Tallahassee ★ (10) Jacksonville
Apalachicola River
Suwannee River
St. Augustine (95)
(75) (4)
Orlando
Tampa
St. Petersburg
Gulf of Mexico
(75) (95)
Lake Okeechobee West Palm Beach
(75) Miami
Everglades Nat'l Park
Key West • Florida Keys
Atlantic Ocean

Lost in the Swamp

The Everglades is a huge swampy area in southern Florida. You can see lots of interesting plants and animals there. How many of these plants and animals can you find in the puzzle?

CYPRESS
MYRTLES
SNAKES
PELICANS
BAYS
DEER
FISH
WILLOWS
ALLIGATORS
SAWGRASS
PANTHERS
MANGROVES

B	A	J	H	E	K	B	A	D	A
S	W	G	M	Y	R	T	L	E	S
M	I	A	F	D	I	F	W	E	C
A	L	L	I	G	A	T	O	R	S
N	L	G	S	P	E	L	N	R	A
G	O	B	H	E	N	Z	C	H	W
R	W	F	A	L	K	R	C	M	G
O	S	U	N	I	B	A	Y	S	R
V	A	G	Y	C	T	T	P	K	A
E	D	H	W	A	H	N	R	B	S
S	N	P	A	N	T	H	E	R	S
D	Y	K	I	S	B	A	S	N	Y
H	L	S	N	A	K	E	S	R	A

-FOR- REAL! The oldest house in St. Augustine, the oldest city in the U.S., was built about 1703.

Georgia

he Empire State of the South

Brown Thrasher

Cherokee Rose

Legend
- ★ Capital City
- ● City
- [20] Interstate Highway
- National Park
- City Area
- ～ River
- ︿︿ Mountains
- Lake

(Map of Georgia showing: Appalachian Mtns., Blue Ridge Mtns., 75, 85, Atlanta, 20, Stone Mountain, Augusta, 85, Macon, Columbus, 16, Savannah River, Savannah, Flint River, 75, Waycross, 95, Valdosta, Okefenokee Swamp)

Compass: N, NE, E, SE, S, SW, W, NW

0 25 50 75 100
miles

Fore!

The Masters Golf Tournament is held in Augusta. In this Masters Tournament the golf balls have really been flying! Can you find 12 hidden golf balls?

MAP ✓
How far is Atlanta from the northern border of Georgia?

TO SIRRELL

-FOR- REAL!
Georgia is often called the Goober State because it produces more goobers than any other state. (For all you Northerners, goobers are peanuts.)

Hawaii

The Aloha State

Nene

Yellow Hibiscus

Niihau

Kauai

Oahu
Kailua
Pearl Harbor
Honolulu

Molokai

Lanai
Kahului
Haleakala Nat'l Park

Kahoolawe
Maui

Pacific Ocean

Pacific Ocean

Hawaii
Hilo
Hawaii Volcanoes Nat'l Park

MAP ✔

How many main islands make up the state of Hawaii?

Nui (Great) Puzzle

Aloha (welcome)! Are you **akamai** (clever)? **Ae** (yes) or **aole** (no)? The Hawaiian alphabet has only 12 letters. You can see them on the leaves of the pineapple. How quickly can you fill the boxes on the pineapple with words made from these letters?

L H I E A
K
M
N
O
P U W

-FOR- REAL! Hawaii is a chain of 132 islands that extends 1,523 miles.

Idaho

The Gem State

Mountain Bluebird

Syringa

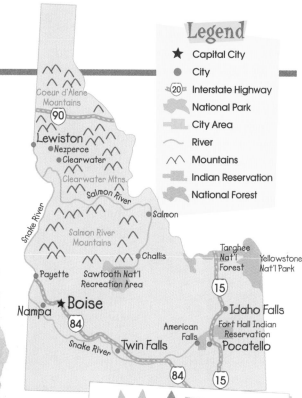

Legend

- ★ Capital City
- ● City
- 20 Interstate Highway
- National Park
- City Area
- ～ River
- ⋀ Mountains
- Indian Reservation
- National Forest

Sack Race

Idaho and potatoes go together like, well, Idaho potatoes! Play this Idaho potato sack race with another player. You need four coins (two to toss and two to move along the game board). Heads takes the first turn. Move 1 space for heads and 2 for tails. The first player to reach the baked potato wins.

MAP ✔

What is Idaho's capital and largest city? How can you tell?

-FOR- REAL! Crystal Ice Cave, near American Falls, has a frozen waterfall and a frozen river.

Illinois

ILLINOIS

The Prairie State

Cardinal

Purple Violet

All About Abe 1¢

Solve the crossword puzzle. Use these words if you need help.

REPUBLICAN	ILLINOIS	SIXTEENTH	CIVIL WAR
MARY TODD	LAWYER	KENTUCKY	SECEDED
HONEST ABE	ASSASSINATED		

Across

5. the state where Lincoln lived for 25 years
7. Lincoln was our ___ president.
8. Lincoln's profession
9. Lincoln was ___ on April 4, 1865.
10. The Confederate states ___ from the Union.

Down

1. Lincoln's political party when he was elected president
2. Lincoln's nickname
3. the state where Lincoln was born
4. the war that was fought during Lincoln's presidency
6. the name of Lincoln's wife

-FOR- REAL!

In Chicago, people say that everyone is Irish on St. Patrick's Day. One way Chicagoans celebrate is by dyeing the Chicago River green!

MAP ✓

Do more people live in northern Illinois or southern Illinois? Why do you think so?

Indiana

The Hoosier State

Cardinal

Peony

MAP ✓

Which highways go through the state capital?

Hammond
Lake Michigan
Gary — 90 — South Bend — 80
Fort Wayne
65
Wabash River
69
Lafayette
74
Indianapolis ★
70
70
74
White River
Wabash River
65
Hoosier Nat'l Forest
Evansville
Ohio River

The Indy 500!

The place: Indianapolis
The date: Memorial Day
The event: The Indianapolis 500 auto race

Which car will make it to the finish line?

Legend
★ Capital City
● City
20 Interstate Highway
National Forest
City Area
River

FINISH

-FOR-REAL! Play ball! The first professional baseball league game was played on May 4, 1871, in Fort Wayne.

Iowa

The Hawkeye State

Eastern Goldfinch

Wild Rose

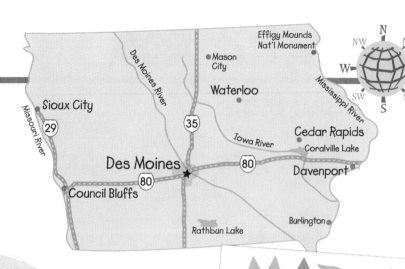

Effigy Mounds Nat'l Monument
Mason City
Des Moines River
Waterloo
Sioux City
Missouri River
29
35
Iowa River
Cedar Rapids
Coralville Lake
Mississippi River
Des Moines
80
80
Davenport
Council Bluffs
Burlington
Rathbun Lake

Corny

Cornfields and more cornfields—that's what you see in Iowa, producer of more corn than any other state. Take a look at the ears of corn. They may all look alike at first, but they aren't. Find the ear of corn that is different from the rest.

MAP ✔

Which river borders Iowa on the west? On the east?

-FOR-REAL!

Iowa has a higher percentage of people who can read and write than any other state.

Kansas

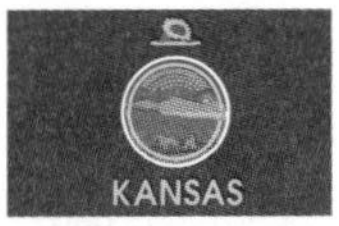

KANSAS

The Sunflower State

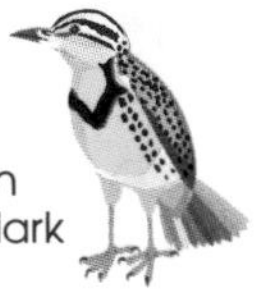

Western Meadowlark

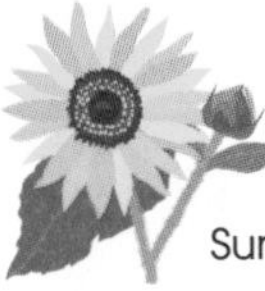

Sunflower

Missouri River
Tuttle Creek Lake
Milford Lake
Fort Riley Military Area
Perry Lake
Leavenworth
Kansas City
Saline River
Smoky Hill River
70
Abilene
Topeka
335
135
35
Arkansas River
Dodge City
Wichita
Argonia
35
0 20 40 60 80 100
miles

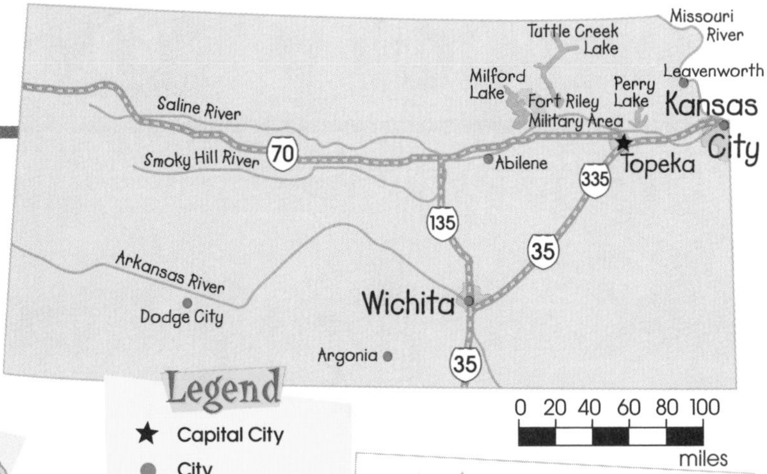

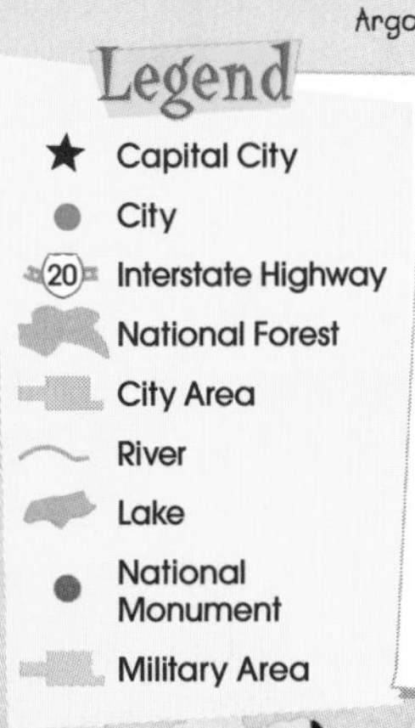

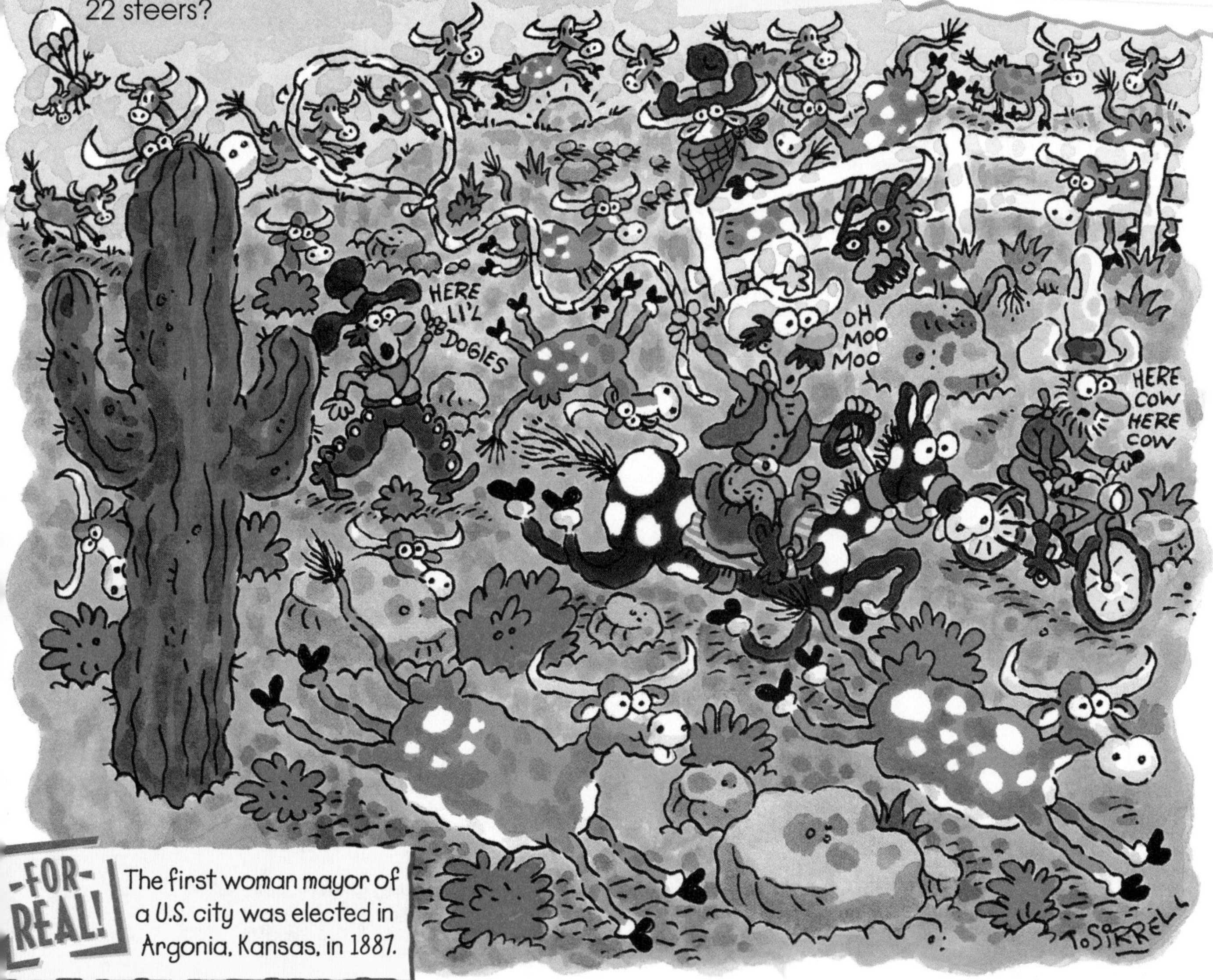

Legend
Capital City
City
20 Interstate Highway
National Forest
City Area
River
Lake
National Monument
Military Area

MAP ✓

How many miles is Wichita from the southern border of the state?

Get Along Little Dogies!

In the 1860s and 1870s, cowboys herded cattle from Texas to Dodge City and other Kansas towns to be shipped all over the U.S. These longhorns just stampeded! Help the cowboys gather the herd. Can you find all 22 steers?

HERE LI'L DOGIES
OH MOO MOO
HERE COW HERE COW

FOR REAL! The first woman mayor of a U.S. city was elected in Argonia, Kansas, in 1887.

Kentucky

COMMONWEALTH OF KENTUCKY

The Bluegrass State

Kentucky Cardinal

Goldenrod

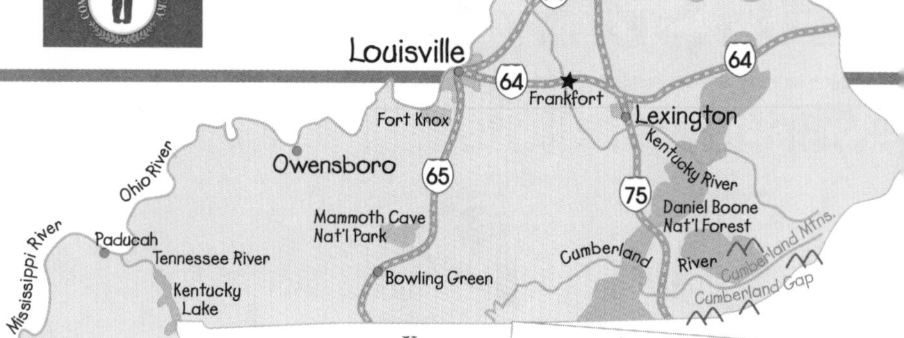

Ohio River
71
Louisville
64
Frankfort
64
Lexington
Fort Knox
Owensboro
65
Ohio River
Kentucky River
75
Daniel Boone Nat'l Forest
Mammoth Cave Nat'l Park
Mississippi River
Paducah
Tennessee River
Kentucky Lake
Bowling Green
Cumberland River
Cumberland Mtns.
Cumberland Gap

N
NE
E
SE
S
SW
W
NW

MAP

Which interstate highway connects Louisville and Lexington?

Derby Days

Kentucky is known for its beautiful thoroughbred racehorses. Do you know the name of the most famous racehorse of all? Crack the code to find out. Cross off all the vowels except **o**. Then write the letter of the alphabet that comes before each of the letters that are left.

eiiauNeebuuao ieep' eiXiabaase

T. SIRRELL

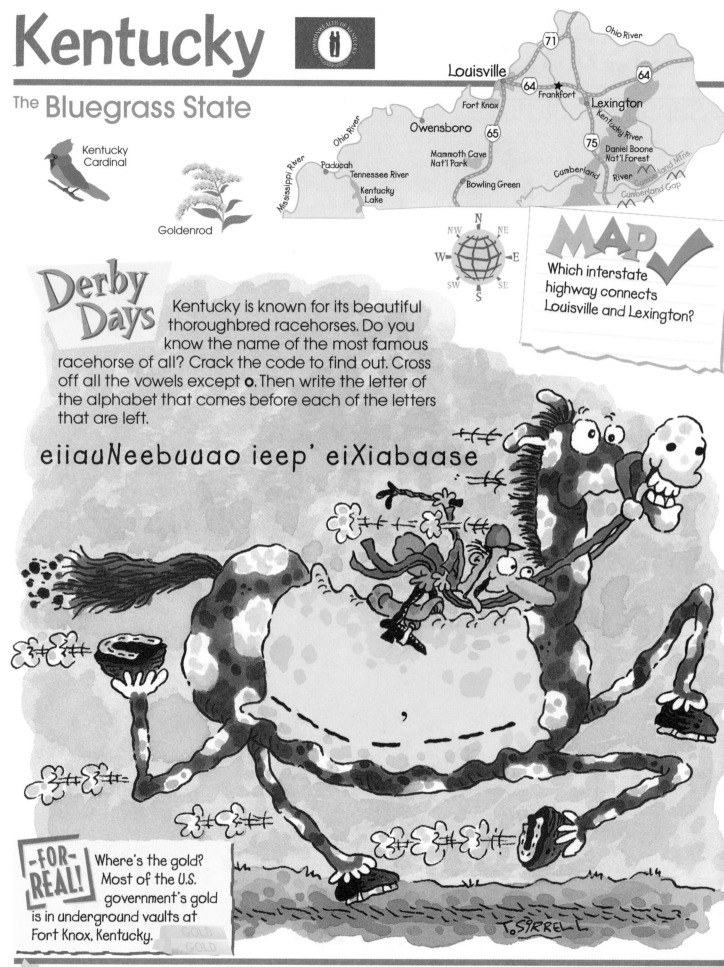

FOR REAL! Where's the gold? Most of the U.S. government's gold is in underground vaults at Fort Knox, Kentucky.

Louisiana

The Pelican State

Brown Pelican

Magnolia

UNION, JUSTICE & CONFIDENCE

Legend
- ★ Capital City
- ● City
- 20 Interstate Highway
- National Park
- City Area
- River
- Mountains
- Military Area
- National Forest
- Lake

Map labels: 20 Monroe · Shreveport · Kisatchie Nat'l Forest · Kisatchie Nat'l Forest · Red River · Mississippi River · Fort Polk Military Area · 49 · Baton Rouge · 12 · Lake Pontchartrain · 10 · Lake Charles · Lafayette · 10 · Mississippi River · New Orleans · Gulf of Mexico

Let's Party!

Every year, New Orleans hosts a wild celebration called Mardi Gras, complete with parties, parades, jazz, and costumes. Look at the Mardi Gras masks. How many pairs of matching masks can you find?

MAP ✓
Which two rivers are on the map?

Bourbon Street

-FOR- REAL!
In 1803, the U.S. bought Louisiana from France for $15 million. Imagine what Louisiana would cost today!

Maine

The Pine Tree State

Chickadee

White Pine Cone and Tassel

NW N NE
W E
SW SE
S

St. John River

Moosehead Lake

Mount Katahdin
elv. 5,268 ft

Penobscot River

Kennebec River

Passamaquo

95 Bangor

Waterville

★ Augusta

Acadia Nat'l Park
Mount Desert Island

Lewiston

495

Atlantic Ocean

Portland

95

Search a Forest

How many of these trees that grow in Maine can you find?

BASSWOOD
HEMLOCK
SPRUCE
BEECH
MAPLE
BIRCH
PINE
OAK
FIR

MAP ✓

Which part of Maine has the fewest towns and highways: the north or the south?

C	P	I	N	E	B	H	D	R	H
E	H	M	A	P	A	F	B	S	K
B	E	E	C	H	S	A	I	P	E
K	L	I	M	A	S	B	R	R	E
O	C	H	E	L	W	E	C	U	B
M	A	P	L	E	O	S	H	C	F
C	B	K	U	K	O	C	P	E	R
L	S	I	P	C	D	W	K	M	U
D	P	U	N	B	I	R	N	H	M

-FOR- REAL! Since forests cover 90% of the state, forest products are important to Maine's economy. Do you know which wood product Maine manufactures more of than all the other states? It's toothpicks!

Maryland

The Old Line State

Baltimore Oriole

Black-Eyed Susan

Legend

- ★ Capital City
- ● City
- 20 Interstate Highway
- City Area
- ～ River
- ⋀⋀ Mountains
- Lake
- National Park

Cumberland • Hagerstown
Appalachian Mtns
68
Potomac River
83 Susquehanna River 95
70
270 Silver Spring 95 Baltimore
Bethesda Annapolis ★
Chesapeake Bay
Potomac River

Day & Knight

Use the code to learn the name of Maryland's official sport.

■	= s
✳	= j
★	= u
▲	= o
✖	= g
●	= t
◉	= n
♠	= i

MAP ✓

What is the name of the bay that almost cuts Maryland into two parts?

✳ ▲ ★ ■ ● ♠ ◉ ✖

-FOR-REAL! The first American steam engine, The Tom Thumb, operated in Baltimore in 1830.

Massachusetts

The Bay State

Chickadee

Mayflower

Merrimack River
Lowell
Concord
Salem
Cambridge
Boston
Quincy
Worcester
Connecticut River
Housatonic River
Springfield
Cape Cod
Cape Cod Bay
Fall River
Nantucket Sound
Martha's Vineyard
91
90
93
95
495
N
NE
NW
W
SW
SE
S

Search the Stars

Find out two famous Massachusetts firsts. Start at the ▼ and write every other letter to learn one. Start at the ▼ to learn the other.

P W O O S R T L O D F S F E I R C I E E S S

MAP ✓

How many interstate highways go into Boston?

-FOR- REAL! Which witch? The Salem witch trial of 1692 resulted in the deaths of 19 innocent people.

Michigan

The Wolverine State

Robin

Apple Blossom

Michigan Squared

Can you solve the Michigan crossword puzzle? Use these words.

CEREAL	FRUIT	LANSING
WOLVERINE	EAGLE	MOTOR CITY
TOURISTS	TWO	FOUR

[Map of Michigan with labeled cities: Isle Royale Nat'l Park, Copper Harbor, Lake Superior, Ironwood, Marquette, Munising, Pictured Rocks Nat'l Lakeshore, Sault Ste. Marie, Escanaba, Manistique, Straits of Mackinac, Mackinac Island, Manitou Islands, Alpena, Lake Huron, Traverse City, Manistee Nat'l Forest, Saginaw, Muskegon, Grand River, Flint, Grand Haven, Grand Rapids, Lansing, Kalamazoo, Ann Arbor, Detroit, Lake Erie, Lake Michigan]

Legend

★ Capital City
● City
(20) Interstate Highway
National Park
City Area
River
National Forest

MAP ✓

Which Great Lakes border Michigan?

Across

3. the nickname of Detroit, the country's leading car manufacturing city
5. the bird on Michigan's state flag
6. Michigan is famous for its apples and other kinds of ___.
8. the capital of Michigan
9. The state of Michigan has ___ parts.

Down

1. the animal in Michigan's motto
2. the number of Great Lakes that border Michigan
4. Battle Creek is the home of Kellogg and other ___ makers.
7. Michigan's scenic beauty attracts many ___ every year.

-FOR- REAL! Besides the Great Lakes, Michigan has more than 11,000 smaller lakes.

Minnesota

The Gopher State

Common Loon

Pink and White Lady's Slipper

Map of Minnesota showing: Rainy Lake, Upper Red Lake, Lower Red Lake, Mesabi Iron Range, Superior Nat'l Forest, White Earth Indian Reservation, Winnibigoshish Lake, Hibbing, Lake Superior, Leech Lake, Duluth, Moorhead, Red River of the North, Mississippi River, Mille Lacs Lake, 94, 35, St. Cloud, Stillwater, Minneapolis, Minnesota River, St. Paul, Mississippi River, 35, 90

Compass: N, NE, E, SE, S, SW, W, NW

Scale: 0 20 40 60 miles

Can You Canoe?

Visitors love Minnesota's thousands of beautiful lakes and rivers. Help this voyager find the route to **portage**, or carry, her canoe to the lake.

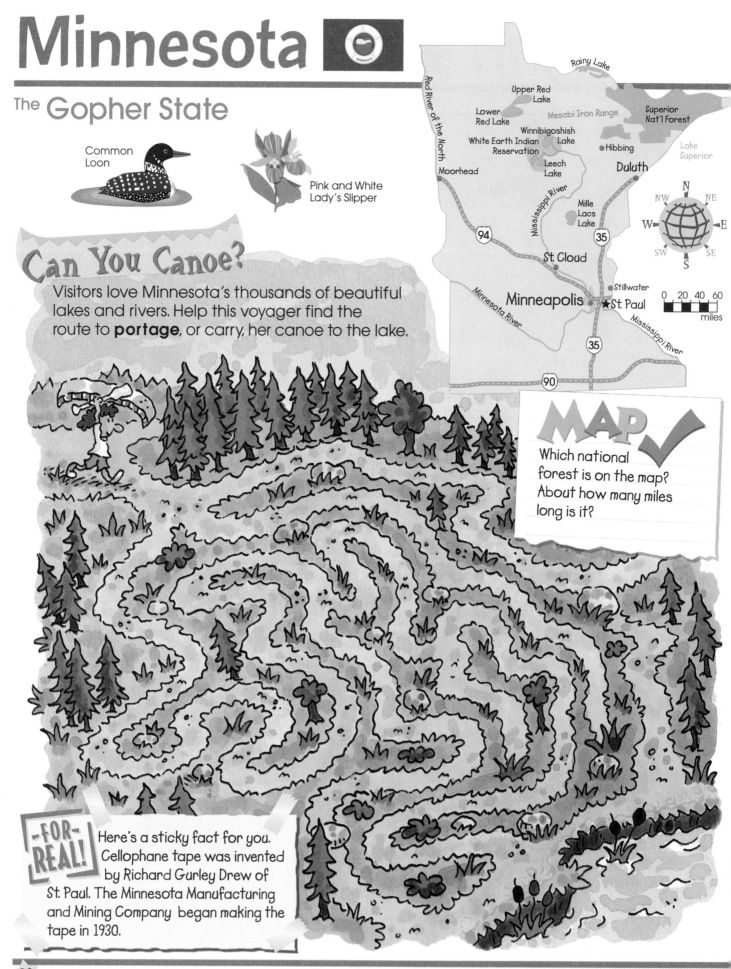

MAP ✓

Which national forest is on the map? About how many miles long is it?

-FOR- REAL!

Here's a sticky fact for you. Cellophane tape was invented by Richard Gurley Drew of St. Paul. The Minnesota Manufacturing and Mining Company began making the tape in 1930.

Mississippi

the Magnolia State

Mockingbird

Magnolia

M-i-s-s-i-s-s-i-p-p-i Means What!?

Write the letters coming from the smoke stack in reverse order. Then cross off every third letter to find out what **Mississippi**, an early Indian name, means.

_____

Legend
- ★ Capital City
- ● City
- 🛣 20 Interstate Highway
- National Forest
- City Area
- River
- Mountains
- Indian Reservation

Holly Springs Nat'l Forest

Tombigbee River

Clarksdale

Holly Springs Nat'l Forest

Mississippi River

Big Sunflower River

Big Black River

55

Pearl River

Vicksburg

Meridian

Jackson ★

20

59

55

Pearl River

Natchez

Hattiesburg

0 10 20 30 40 50 miles

Biloxi

10   Gulfport

MAP ✔

About how many miles is it from Gulfport to Biloxi?

reftaiwtpaeorg

-FOR- REAL!

The first heart transplant was performed in 1964 at the University of Mississippi Medical Center.

Missouri

The Show Me State

Bluebird

Hawthorn

St. Joseph

Kansas City

Independence   Columbia

Jefferson City ★

Missouri River

St. Louis

Springfield

Mark Twain Nat'l Forest

Mark Twain Nat'l Forest

0 20 40 60 80 100
miles

Sweet Dreams!

Ice cream cones were first served at the 1904 World's Fair in St. Louis. This boy is dreaming of ice cream cones. Circle the two cones that are exactly alike.

MAP ✓

Is Springfield closer to Kansas City or St. Louis?

FOR REAL! The Gateway Arch in St. Louis is the tallest monument in the U.S.

Montana

Treasure State

Western Meadowlark

Bitter Root

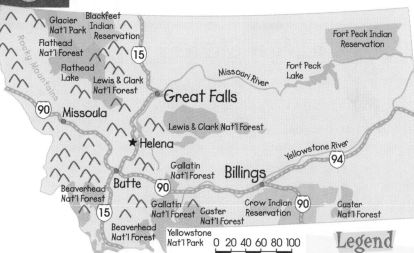

Glacier Nat'l Park
Blackfeet Indian Reservation
Fort Peck Indian Reservation
Flathead Nat'l Forest
Rocky Mountains
15
Flathead Lake
Lewis & Clark Nat'l Forest
Missouri River
Fort Peck Lake
90 Missoula
Great Falls
Lewis & Clark Nat'l Forest
★ Helena
Yellowstone River
94
Gallatin Nat'l Forest
Billings
Butte
90
Beaverhead Nat'l Forest
Gallatin Nat'l Forest
Custer Nat'l Forest
Crow Indian Reservation
90
Custer Nat'l Forest
15
Beaverhead Nat'l Forest
Yellowstone Nat'l Park
0 20 40 60 80 100 miles

Legend
- ★ Capital City
- ● City
- 20 Interstate Highway
- National Park
- City Area
- ∿ River
- ∧∧ Mountains
- Indian Reservation
- National Forest
- Lake

GOLD   COAL   CATTLE   BILLINGS
SILVER SKY   GLACIER   CANADA
FOURTH HELENA MOUNTAINS

MAP ✓ How many national parks and forests are on the map?

Across

3. Montana has many tall, rugged ___.
5. It lies north of Montana.
6. Montana is the ___ largest state.
8. Montana's largest city
9. one of the minerals mined in Montana
10. On Montana's vast plains, ___ graze on grass.

Down

1. This popular national park is located in northwest Montana.
2. one of the minerals that give Montana its nickname
4. Montana is often called "Big ___ Country."
5. Montana's most important mining product
7. the capital of Montana

-FOR-REAL! In 1916, Jeanette Rankin of Missoula became the first woman representative to the U.S. Congress.

Nebraska

The Cornhusker State

Western Meadowlark

Goldenrod

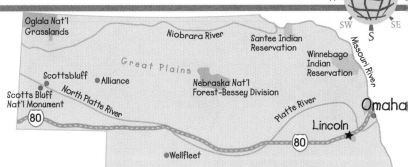

Oglala Nat'l Grasslands
Niobrara River
Santee Indian Reservation
Great Plains
Winnebago Indian Reservation
Missouri River
Scottsbluff • Alliance
Nebraska Nat'l Forest-Bessey Division
North Platte River
Scotts Bluff Nat'l Monument
80
Platte River
Lincoln
80
Omaha
• Wellfleet

Wildlife Search

Here are some plants and animals you might see in Nebraska. How many can you find in the puzzle?

- PHEASANTS
- PERCH
- TROUT
- LARKSPURS
- RABBITS
- SKUNKS
- BADGERS
- COTTONWOODS
- CEDARS
- DUCKS
- PIKE
- CHOKECHERRIES
- POPPIES
- RACCOONS
- GEESE
- COYOTES
- PINES
- HACKBERRIES

MAP ✓

On which side of the state is Omaha?

C	O	Y	O	T	E	S	H	U	P
C	S	D	U	C	K	S	R	N	I
O	L	O	P	C	B	A	C	L	K
T	R	A	E	H	U	P	E	H	E
T	A	N	R	O	I	S	D	A	S
O	B	R	C	K	E	O	A	C	G
N	B	A	H	E	S	O	R	K	P
W	I	C	G	C	M	P	S	B	H
O	T	C	U	H	B	O	U	E	E
O	S	O	D	E	I	P	T	R	A
D	R	O	O	R	E	P	L	R	S
S	N	N	W	R	S	I	Y	I	A
Y	M	S	P	I	N	E	S	E	N
B	A	D	G	E	R	S	O	S	T
N	K	Y	O	S	K	U	N	K	S

-FOR- REAL! What a mammoth mammoth! The biggest mammoth fossil ever discovered was dug up near Wellfleet in 1922.

Nevada

The Silver State

Mountain Bluebird

Sagebrush

Nevada Info

Fill in the blanks. Then write the letters with numbers under them in the boxes to learn what Nevada gets less of than any other state.

MINES   FORESTS   LAKE MEAD   HOOVER DAM

SILVER   CACTUS   LAS VEGAS   RENO

1. a beautiful lake in the mountains __ __ __ __ __ __ __ __ __
                                      8

2. a common desert plant __ __ __ __ __ __
                             2

3. a shiny gray metal __ __ __ __ __ __
                         3

4. Lots of gambling goes on here. __ __ __ __ __ __ __ __ __
                                      7

5. It provides water and electricity, too. __ __ __ __ __ __ __ __ __
                                                              6

6. Pine __ cover many mountains here. __ __ __ __ __ __ __
                                         5

7. another city where people go to gamble __ __ __ __
                                             1

8. There are still silver and gold __ in Nevada. __ __ __ __ __ __
                                                         4

MAP ✓

What is the name of the military area in Nevada? In what part of the state is it located?

Legend

★ Capital City
● City
⑳ Interstate Highway
National Park
City Area
River
Mountains
Indian Reservation
National Forest
Lake
Military Area
● National Monument

Map labels: Independence Mtns., 80, Pyramid Lake Indian Res., 80, Pyramid Lake, Reno, Shoshone Mtns, Egan Range, Lake Tahoe, Sierra Nevada, Virginia City, ★ Carson City, Great Basin, Walker River Indian Res., Great Basin Nat' Park, Walker Lake, Goldfield, Nellis Air Force Range, Death Valley Nat'l Monument, Amargosa Desert, Spring Mtns., Las Vegas, 15, Lake Mead, Hoover Dam, Colorado River

0 20 40 60 80 100 miles

1 2 3 4 5 6 7 8

New Hampshire

The Granite State

It's All Downhill!

Purple Finch

Purple Lilac

Ski down New Hampshire's White Mountains and gather letters along the way. Once you've got them all, you'll have the name of the first American to walk in space. (He's from New Hampshire, of course!)

White Mountains

White Mountain Nat'l Forest

White Mountain Nat'l Forest

Connecticut River

White Mountains

93

Lake Winnipesaukee

Merrimack River

89

Connecticut River

★ Concord

Manchester

Portsmouth

Nashua

93

MAP ✓

On which river is Concord?

FOR REAL! The Navy's first shipbuilding yard opened in 1800 in Portsmouth. It built warships in WWI and submarines in WWII.

To SIRRELL

_ _ _ _ _ _ _ _ _ _ _ _ , _

New Jersey

The Garden State

Eastern Goldfinch

Purple Violet

Legend
★ Capital City
● City
20 Interstate Highway
National Forest
City Area
River
Mountains
Lake

N NW NE W E SW SE S

Paterson
Jersey City
Newark
Elizabeth
New Brunswick
Sandy Hook
Piedmont Plateau
Trenton
Fort Dix Military Area
Camden
Atlantic City
Delaware River
Kittatinny Mtns
Hudson River
Coastal Plain
Delaware Bay
Atlantic Ocean
80 287 78 295

Food Fight!

How many names of fruits and vegetables can you find in the Garden State word search? Are you in the mood for some competition? Challenge a friend to see who can find more names in thirty seconds.

TOMATOES   CABBAGES   LETTUCE
POTATOES   SWEET CORN   SNAP BEANS
PEACHES   BLUEBERRIES   GRAPES
CRANBERRIES   SQUASH   PUMPKINS
SWEET POTATOES

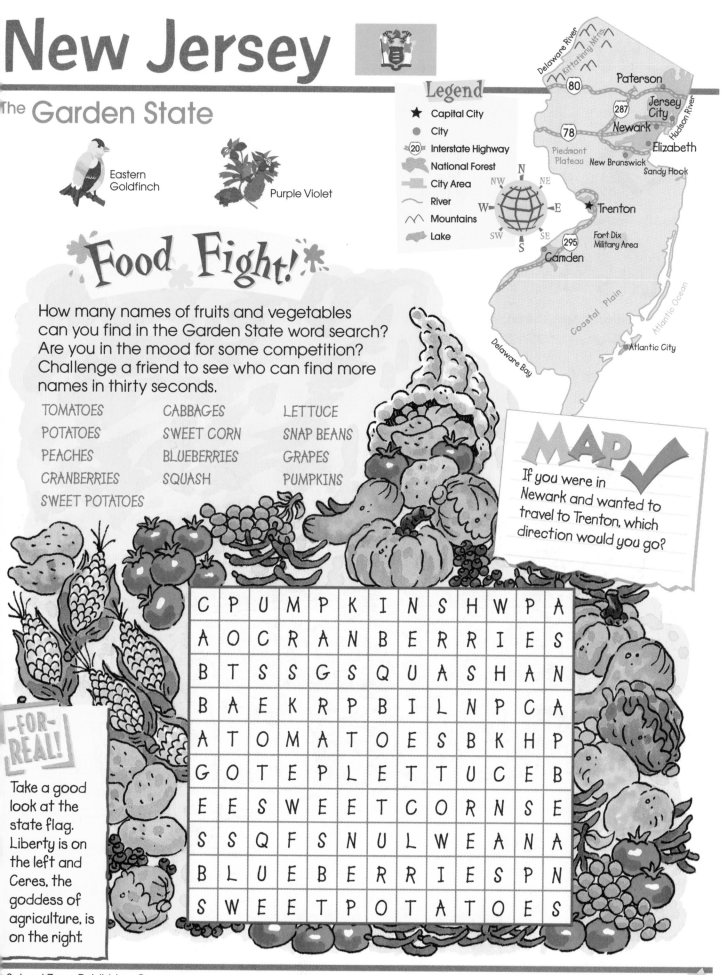

MAP ✓
If you were in Newark and wanted to travel to Trenton, which direction would you go?

C	P	U	M	P	K	I	N	S	H	W	P	A
A	O	C	R	A	N	B	E	R	R	I	E	S
B	T	S	S	G	S	Q	U	A	S	H	A	N
B	A	E	K	R	P	B	I	L	N	P	C	A
A	T	O	M	A	T	O	E	S	B	K	H	P
G	O	T	E	P	L	E	T	T	U	C	E	B
E	E	S	W	E	E	T	C	O	R	N	S	E
S	S	Q	F	S	N	U	L	W	E	A	N	A
B	L	U	E	B	E	R	R	I	E	S	P	N
S	W	E	E	T	P	O	T	A	T	O	E	S

FOR REAL!
Take a good look at the state flag. Liberty is on the left and Ceres, the goddess of agriculture, is on the right.

New Mexico

The Land of Enchantment

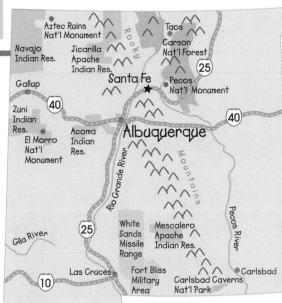

Roadrunner

Yucca Flower

What's the Word?

Some Indians of New Mexico lived in the first apartments. Unscramble the letters on the decorated pots (just the decorated ones) to find out what these buildings are called.

N
NW   NE
W   E
SW   SE
S

MAP ✔

Which highway connects Albuquerque and Santa Fe?

POTS For SALE

-FOR-REAL! New Mexico has a higher percentage of Indians and Hispanics than any other state.

New York

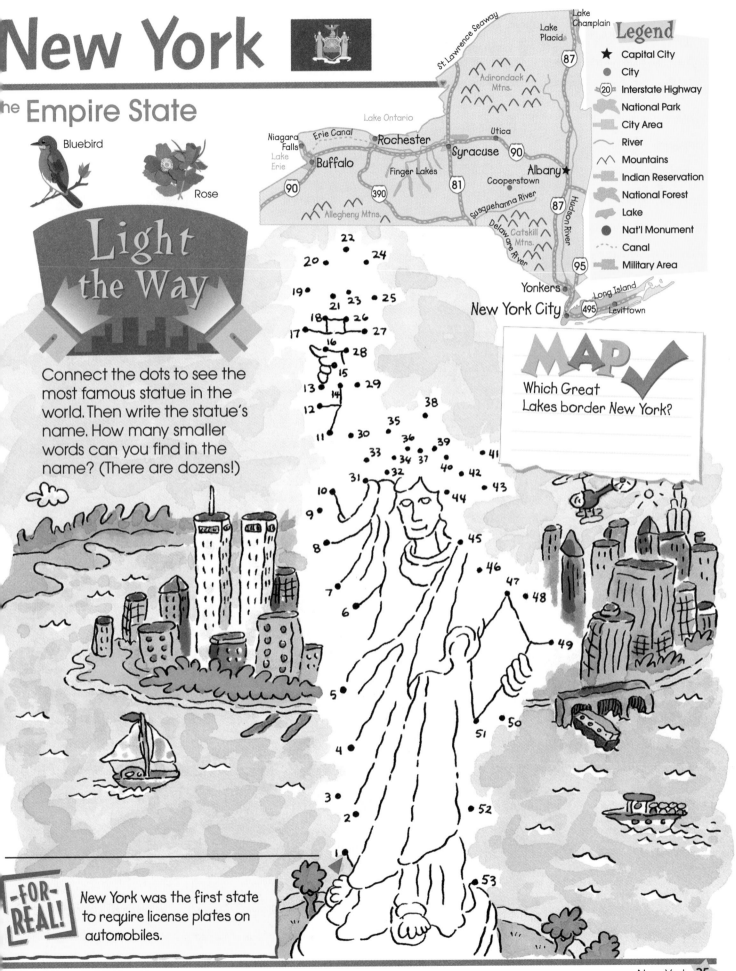

the Empire State

Bluebird

Rose

Light the Way

Connect the dots to see the most famous statue in the world. Then write the statue's name. How many smaller words can you find in the name? (There are dozens!)

Legend

★ Capital City
● City
20 Interstate Highway
National Park
City Area
River
Mountains
Indian Reservation
National Forest
Lake
● Nat'l Monument
Canal
Military Area

Map labels: St. Lawrence Seaway, Lake Placid, Lake Champlain, 87, Adirondack Mtns., Lake Ontario, Erie Canal, Niagara Falls, Rochester, Utica, Syracuse, 90, Lake Erie, Buffalo, Finger Lakes, 81, Cooperstown, Albany ★, 90, 390, Allegheny Mtns., Susquehanna River, Delaware River, Catskill Mtns., Hudson River, 87, 95, Yonkers, New York City, 495, Long Island, Levittown

MAP ✓

Which Great Lakes border New York?

-FOR-REAL!
New York was the first state to require license plates on automobiles.

© School Zone Publishing Company

New York **35**

North Carolina

The Tar Heel State

Cardinal

Flowering Dogwood

Winston-Salem
Greensboro
Durham
Raleigh ★
Charlotte
Asheville
Great Smoky Mtns. Nat'l Park
Blue Ridge Mountains
Piedmont Region
85
40
77
85
95
Coastal Plains
Dismal Swamp
Kitty Hawk
Cape Hatteras
Atlantic Ocean
40
Wilmington

N NE NW W E SW S SE

Shipwreck!

Off North Carolina's shore lies Cape Hatteras, known as the graveyard of the Atlantic. No one knows how many ships have gone down in these rough seas. What can you find in this shipwreck? Circle 19 hidden objects.

MAP ✓

Is the state capital also the largest city?

-FOR- REAL! At Kitty Hawk in 1903, Wilbur and Orville Wright made the first power-driven airplane flight.

North Dakota

the Flickertail State

Western Meadowlark

Wild Praire Rose

T.R.'s Place

What's the name of the area where President Theodore Roosevelt had ranches in the 1880s? (It's a national park and wildlife sanctuary now.) Give up? Cross off these letters to find out: **v, w, x, y, z.**

Turtle Mtns.

Minot

Missouri River

Grand Forks

Red River of the North

Fort Berthold Indian Res.

Theodore Roosevelt Nat'l Park

Lake Sakakawea

Devils Lake Sioux Indian Res.

Missouri River

29

94

Bismarck

Fargo

The Badlands

Great Plains

Standing Rock Indian Res.

Legend

★ Capital City
● City
(20) Interstate Highway
National Park
City Area

~ River
Lake
∧∧ Mountains
Indian Reservation
National Forest

MAP ✔

How many Indian reservations are shown on the map?

T	Z	W	X	Y	V
W	H	V	Y	E	W
Y	X	Z	B	W	X
A	V	D	Y	Y	L
V	A	Y	W	N	Y
W	Z	D	X	S	Z

-FOR- REAL!

Wheat brings in more farm income to North Dakota than any other crop. It's grown in every county in the state.

Ohio

The Buckeye State

 Cardinal

 Scarlet Carnation

Toledo
90
80
Lake Erie
Cleveland
Akron
Youngstown
Canton
75
71
77
Springfield
70
Columbus
Dayton
71
Mound City Group Nat'l Monument
Cincinnati
Wayne National Forest
Ohio River
Ohio River
N NE NW E W SE SW S

Who Did What?

Seven presidents were born in Ohio, more than in any other state. Two famous astronauts were born here. So were three famous inventors. Do you know the presidents from the astronauts? The astronauts from the inventors? Write **p** for president, **a** for astronaut, or **i** for inventor in the boxes.

MAP ✓

Which city on the map is farthest east?

Warren G. Harding ☐

Neil A. Armstrong ☐

William McKinley ☐

William Howard Taft ☐

Ulysses S. Grant ☐

John H. Glenn, Jr. ☐

Orville Wright ☐

Thomas A. Edison ☐

James A. Garfield ☐

Rutherford B. Hayes ☐

Wilbur Wright ☐

Benjamin Harrison ☐

Oklahoma

OKLAHOMA

he Sooner State

Scissor-Tailed Flycatcher

Mistletoe

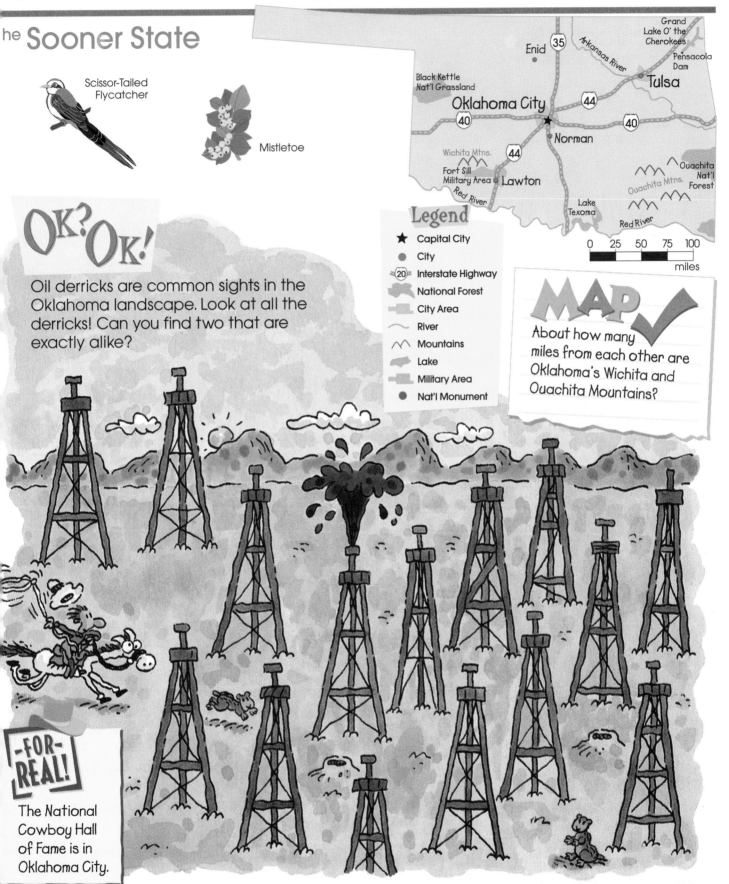

Map

Enid 35
Arkansas River
Grand Lake O' the Cherokees
Black Kettle Nat'l Grassland
Pensacola Dam
Tulsa
Oklahoma City 44
40
40
Norman
Wichita Mtns. 44
Fort Sill Military Area
Lawton
Red River
Ouachita Mtns.
Ouachita Nat'l Forest
Lake Texoma
Red River

Legend

★ Capital City
● City
⑳ Interstate Highway
National Forest
City Area
River
Mountains
Lake
Military Area
● Nat'l Monument

0 25 50 75 100
miles

OK? OK!

Oil derricks are common sights in the Oklahoma landscape. Look at all the derricks! Can you find two that are exactly alike?

MAP ✔

About how many miles from each other are Oklahoma's Wichita and Ouachita Mountains?

FOR REAL!

The National Cowboy Hall of Fame is in Oklahoma City.

Oregon

STATE OF OREGON
1859

The Beaver State

Western Meadowlark

Oregon Grape

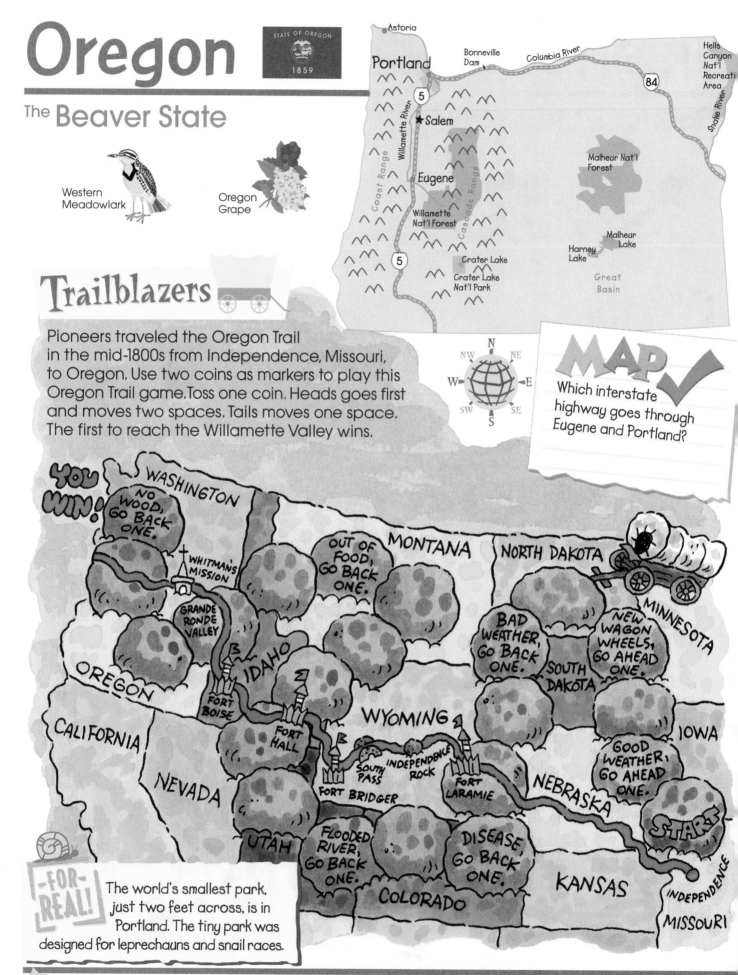

Astoria

Portland

Bonneville Dam

Columbia River

Hells Canyon Nat'l Recreation Area

5

84

Willamette River

Salem

Coast Range

Eugene

Cascade Range

Malheur Nat'l Forest

Willamette Nat'l Forest

5

Crater Lake

Crater Lake Nat'l Park

Harney Lake

Malheur Lake

Great Basin

Snake River

Trailblazers

Pioneers traveled the Oregon Trail in the mid-1800s from Independence, Missouri, to Oregon. Use two coins as markers to play this Oregon Trail game. Toss one coin. Heads goes first and moves two spaces. Tails moves one space. The first to reach the Willamette Valley wins.

N
NW   NE
W   E
SW   SE
S

MAP ✓

Which interstate highway goes through Eugene and Portland?

YOU WIN!

WASHINGTON

NO WOOD, GO BACK ONE.

WHITMAN'S MISSION

GRANDE RONDE VALLEY

OUT OF FOOD, GO BACK ONE.

MONTANA

NORTH DAKOTA

MINNESOTA

BAD WEATHER, GO BACK ONE.

NEW WAGON WHEELS, GO AHEAD ONE.

IDAHO

SOUTH DAKOTA

OREGON

FORT BOISE

FORT HALL

WYOMING

IOWA

CALIFORNIA

SOUTH PASS

INDEPENDENCE ROCK

FORT LARAMIE

GOOD WEATHER, GO AHEAD ONE.

NEVADA

FORT BRIDGER

NEBRASKA

START

UTAH

FLOODED RIVER, GO BACK ONE.

DISEASE, GO BACK ONE.

KANSAS

INDEPENDENCE

COLORADO

MISSOURI

FOR REAL!

The world's smallest park, just two feet across, is in Portland. The tiny park was designed for leprechauns and snail races.

Pennsylvania

The Keystone State

Ruffed Grouse

Mountain Laurel

Barn Art

Some Pennsylvania Dutch farmers paint beautiful designs on their barns. Circle the two Pennsylvania Dutch designs that are exactly the same.

Legend

- ★ Capital City
- ● City
- ⑳ Interstate Highway
- National Park
- City Area
- River
- Lake
- Mountains
- National Forest

MAP ✓

Can you tell from the map whether Pittsburgh is bigger than Philadelphia?

-FOR- REAL!

Yum! The world's largest chocolate factory is in Hershey.

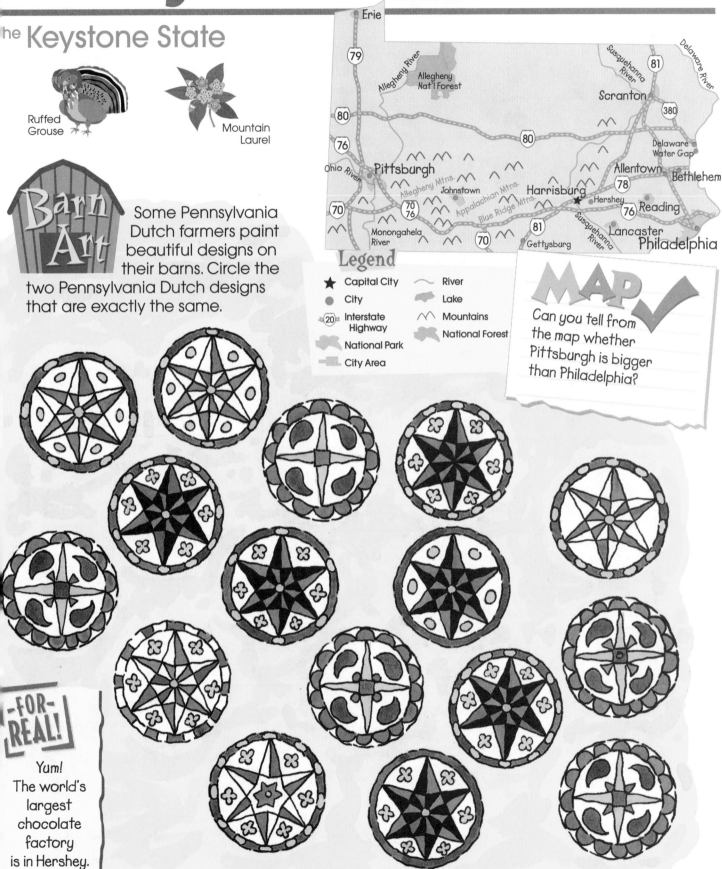

Rhode Island

The Ocean State

Rhode Island Red Chicken

Violet

MAP ✔
How many islands are part of Rhode Island?

Woonsocket

Pawtucket

295

Scituate Reservoir

★ Providence

Providence River

Warwick

95

Prudence Island

Conanicut Island

Narragansett Bay

Island of Rhode Island

Newport

Westerly

Block Island

N
NW   NE
W   E
SW   SE
S

Eggsactly!

Rhode Island Red chickens began the poultry industry in the U.S. These chickens taste great and lay lots of eggs. These Rhode Island Reds have misplaced their eggs! Can you find all 53 eggs?

TOSRRELL

-FOR-REAL!
Rhode Island is the smallest state in the U.S. It is half the size of the next smallest state, Delaware.

South Carolina

The Palmetto State

Carolina Wren

Carolina Jessamine

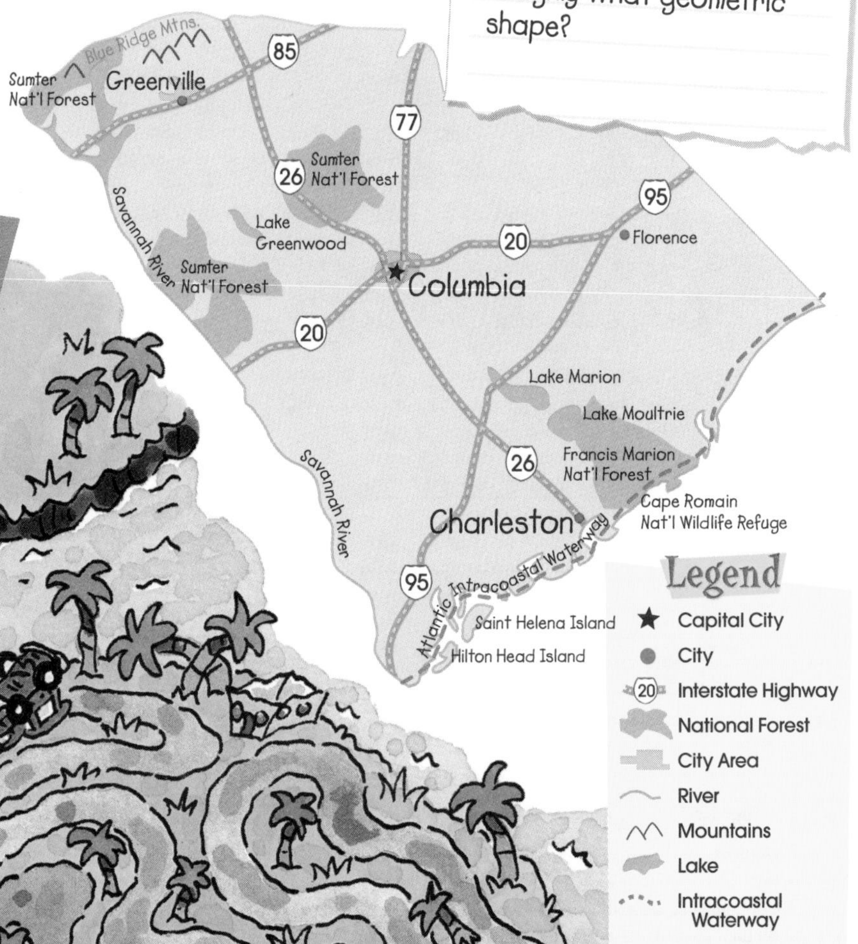

Hazards Ahead!

A hurricane has smashed Saint Helena Island! All the roads off the island are blocked except one. To get off the island, find your way to the bridge.

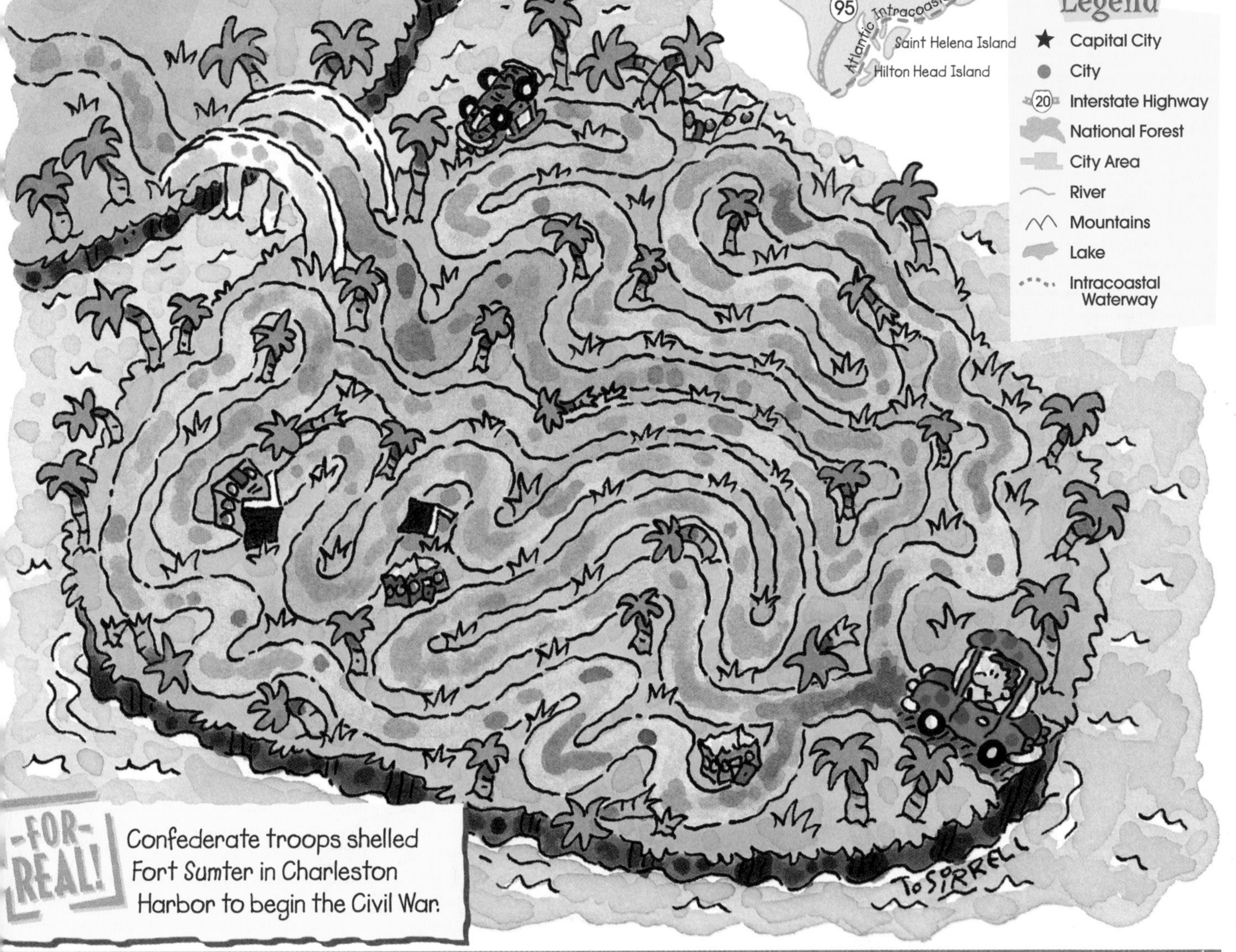

Legend

- ★ Capital City
- ● City
- (20) Interstate Highway
- National Forest
- City Area
- River
- Mountains
- Lake
- Intracoastal Waterway

FOR REAL! Confederate troops shelled Fort Sumter in Charleston Harbor to begin the Civil War.

South Dakota

The Mount Rushmore State

Ring-Necked Pheasant

American Pasqueflower

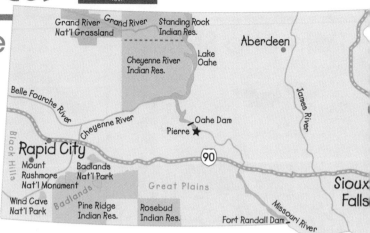

Great Stone Faces

Mount Rushmore pays tribute to which famous Americans?

_____

_____

_____

_____

MAP ✔

How many Indian reservations are shown on this map? Which one is the smallest?

Whose likeness would you add to Mount Rushmore? Sketch that person's portrait.

-FOR-REAL! The geographic center of the U.S. (including Alaska and Hawaii) is in western South Dakota.

Tennessee

The Volunteer State

Mockingbird

Iris

Map

Which mountain ranges are in Tennessee?

Legend

- ★ Capital City
- ● City
- (20) Interstate Highway
- National Park
- City Area
- River
- Mountains
- Indian Reservation
- Lake
- Military Area
- ● Nat'l Monument

On a Clear Day

Wow! You can see seven states from Lookout Mountain. Find their names in the puzzle.

ALABAMA

GEORGIA

SOUTH CAROLINA

NORTH CAROLINA

KENTUCKY

VIRGINIA

TENNESSEE

V	T	E	L	K	N	A	S
H	E	N	T	E	H	P	O
I	N	O	D	N	O	R	U
S	N	R	S	T	V	E	T
A	E	T	U	U	I	R	H
K	S	H	K	C	R	T	C
C	S	C	E	K	G	E	A
G	E	A	T	Y	I	P	R
O	E	R	N	D	N	U	O
H	H	O	Y	O	I	R	L
N	A	L	R	T	A	T	I
I	T	I	N	G	E	L	N
L	V	N	C	K	I	O	A
A	L	A	B	A	M	A	Y

-FOR- REAL! Kingston was the capital of Tennessee for one day, September 21, 1807.

Texas

The Lone Star State

Mockingbird

Bluebonnet

10-Gallon Crossword

Solve the Texas crossword puzzle.

MEXICO   COWBOYS   SECOND   ONE   ALAMO
CATTLE   HOUSTON   AUSTIN   OIL   BLUE

Across

2. It's called liquid gold, and Texas has lots of it.
4. How many stars are on the Texas flag?
5. the state capital
6. They herd cattle across the plains.
10. NASA, headquarters of the U.S. space program, is here.

Down

1. "Remember the ___!"
3. Texas used to be part of this U.S. neighbor to the south.
7. Texas is the ___ largest state.
8. the color of the state flower
9. Texas longhorns are a breed of ___.

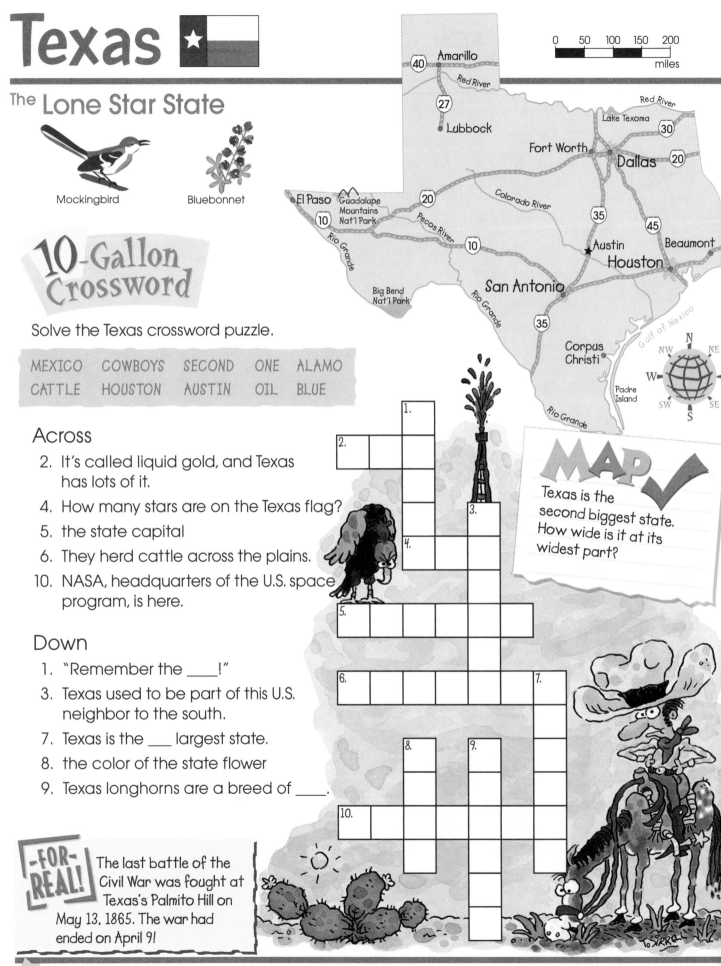

Amarillo
Red River
Lubbock
Fort Worth
Dallas
Lake Texoma
Red River
El Paso
Guadalupe Mountains Nat'l Park
Colorado River
Austin
Houston
Beaumont
Pecos River
San Antonio
Big Bend Nat'l Park
Rio Grande
Corpus Christi
Padre Island
Gulf of Mexico
Rio Grande

miles
0 50 100 150 200

N NE NW W E SW SE S

MAP ✓
Texas is the second biggest state. How wide is it at its widest part?

-FOR-REAL! The last battle of the Civil War was fought at Texas's Palmito Hill on May 13, 1865. The war had ended on April 9!

Utah

The Beehive State

Sea Gull

Sego Lily

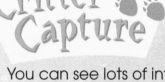
Critter Capture

Legend

★ Capital City
● City
⟨20⟩ Interstate Highway
▨ National Park
▨ City Area
〰 River
⋀⋀ Mountains
▨ Indian Reservation
▨ National Forest
▨ Lake
● Nat'l Monument

Map labels:
Great Salt Lake
⟨84⟩ Ogden
Great Salt Lake Desert
Wasatch Range
⟨80⟩
★ Salt Lake City
Wasatch-Cache Nat'l Forest
Rocky Mtns.
Ashley Nat'l Forest
Great Basin
● Provo
Uintah & Ouray Indian Res.
Ashley Nat'l Forest
⟨15⟩
⟨70⟩
Arches Nat'l Park
Colorado River
Fishlake Nat'l Forest
Canyonlands Nat'l Park
⟨15⟩
Bryce Canyon Nat'l Park
Lake Powell
Natural Bridges Monument
Zion Nat'l Park
Glen Canyon Nat'l Recreation Area
● Rainbow Bridge Nat'l Monument

You can see lots of interesting animals in Utah. Can you identify the ones below? Write the numbers in the boxes.

1. TROUT
2. BADGER
3. BLACK BEAR
4. COYOTE
5. GOOSE
6. MOOSE
7. TORTOISE
8. PHEASANT
9. SKUNK
10. WEASEL
11. MULE DEER
12. MOUNTAIN LION
13. RABBIT
14. BUFFALO
15. PRONGHORN SHEEP

MAP ✓

Which interstate highway goes just south of the Great Salt Lake?

-FOR- REAL!

Salt Lake City has a monument to honor the sea gull, the state bird. Sea gulls saved crops in the area from being eaten by crickets in 1848. How? The gulls ate the crickets!

Vermont

The Green Mountain State

Hermit Thrush

Red Clover

Downhill Racers

Vermont's Green Mountains are a wonderful place to ski! Help this skier choose the shortest path down the mountain.

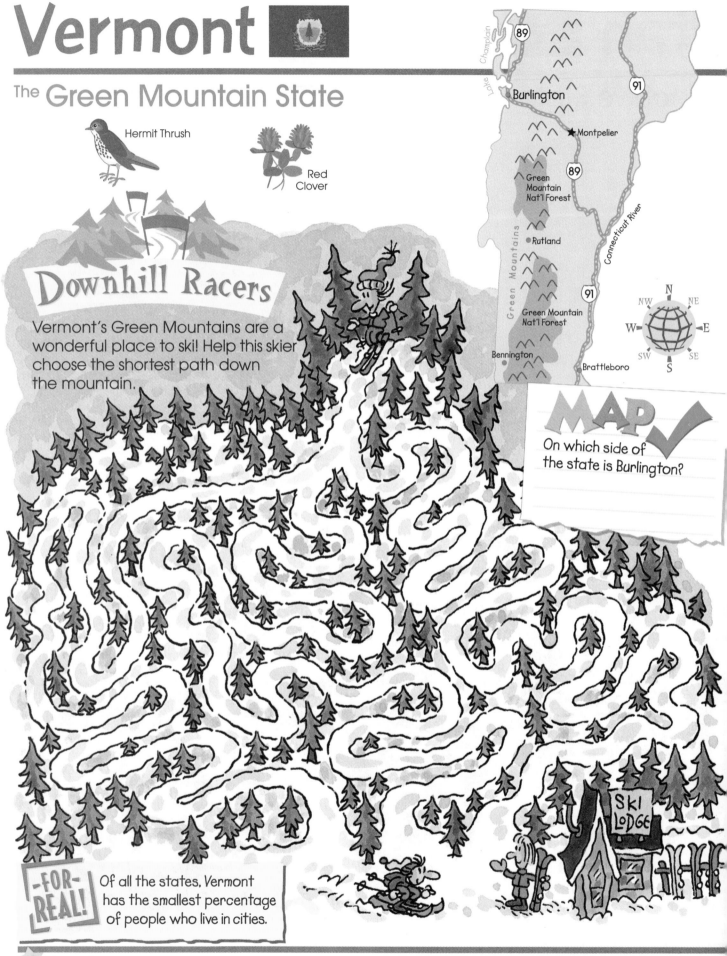

MAP ✓

On which side of the state is Burlington?

SKI LODGE

-FOR-REAL! Of all the states, Vermont has the smallest percentage of people who live in cities.

Lake Champlain

89

91

Burlington

★ Montpelier

89

Green Mountain Nat'l Forest

Rutland

Green Mountains

Connecticut River

91

Green Mountain Nat'l Forest

Bennington

Brattleboro

N NE NW E W SW SE S

Virginia

The Old Dominion State

Cardinal

Flowering Dogwood

Shenandoah Nat'l Park · Arlington · 66 · Shenandoah River · Rappahannock River · Potomac River · Chesapeake Bay · 64 · 95 · **Richmond** ★ · Williamsburg · 64 · James River · Roanoke · 81 · Blue Ridge Mtns. · Appalachian Mtns. · Piedmont Region · Newport News · Portsmouth · 85 · Norfolk · Virginia Beach · Cumberland Gap · Dismal Swamp

A Long, Long Time Ago

Williamsburg has been restored to look as it used to in colonial times. In this picture, Williamsburg looks as it did in the 1700s. Or does it? Circle the modern things in the picture.

MAP ✓

Which part of the state has the biggest cities?

Legend

★ Capital City
● City
20 Interstate Highway
National Park
City Area
River
Mountains
National Forest

-FOR- REAL! Tourists still visit Mount Vernon, the home of George Washington, and Monticello, Thomas Jefferson's home in Virginia.

Washington

The Evergreen State

Willow Goldfinch

Coast Rhododendron

Ross Dam
North Cascades Nat'l Park
Colville Nat'l Forest
Colville Indian Res.
Columbia River
5
Olympic Mtns.
Olympic Nat'l Park
Puget Sound
Wenatchee Nat'l Forest
Grand Coulee Dam
Spokane
Seattle
Cascade Tunnel
Coastal Range
North Pacific Ocean
Tacoma
90
Olympia ★
Mt. Rainier
Mount Rainier Nat'l Park
Snake River
5
Cascade Range
Mt. St. Helens
Yakima Indian Res.
Richland • Walla Walla
Vancouver
Bonneville Dam
Columbia River

0 20 40 60 80 10
mile

Crack the Orchard Code!

Washington grows more of this fruit than any other state does. It is also a top producer of another fruit. Start at the ▼ and write every fourth letter on the outside circle to find out the first fruit. Write every third letter on the inner circle to find out the second fruit.

MAP ✓

How many miles is it from Spokane to Seattle?

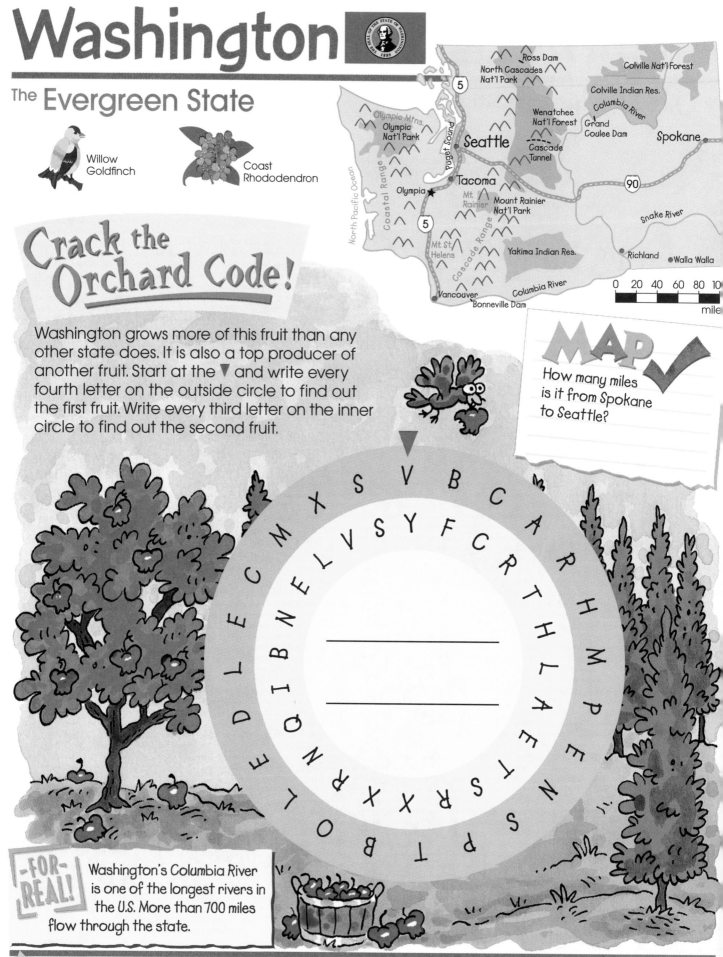

FOR REAL! Washington's Columbia River is one of the longest rivers in the U.S. More than 700 miles flow through the state.

West Virginia

the Mountain State

Cardinal

Rhododendron

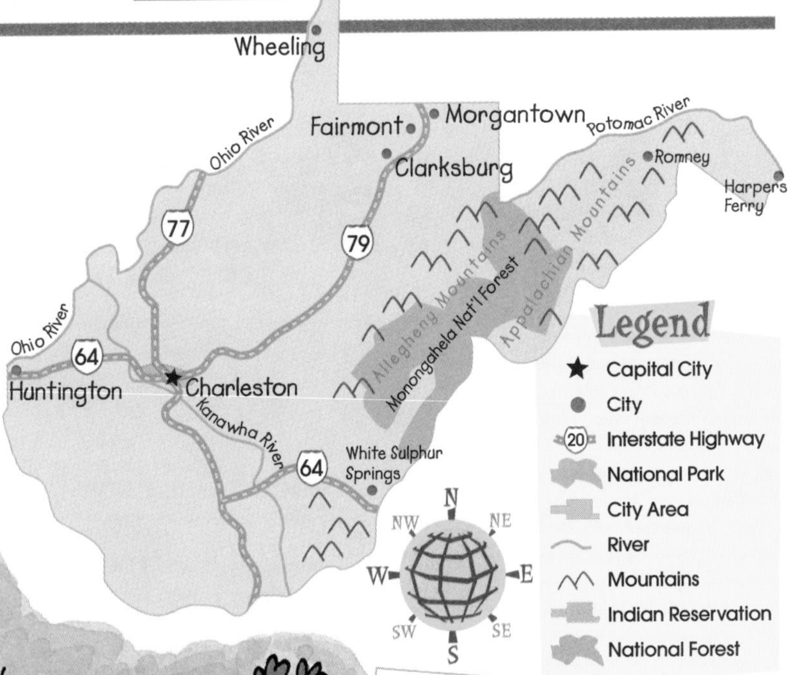

Uphill & Down

Take a hike through the Mountain State. Draw yourself and some friends. Then color the rest of the picture.

Legend

★ Capital City
● City
(20) Interstate Highway
National Park
City Area
River
Mountains
Indian Reservation
National Forest

Weirton
Wheeling
Fairmont
Morgantown
Clarksburg
Romney
Harpers Ferry
Ohio River
Potomac River
Alleghany Mountains
Appalachian Mountains
Monongahela Nat'l Forest
77
79
64
64
Huntington
Charleston
White Sulphur Springs
Kanawha River
Ohio River

N
NE
NW
E
W
SE
SW
S

MAP ✓

Which city is the farthest west? East?

-FOR- REAL! During the Civil War, the town of Romney changed hands between the Union and the Confederacy 56 times!

Wisconsin

The Badger State

Robin

Wood Violet

N
NW NE
W E
SW SE
S

Lake Superior

Lac Courte Oreilles · Lake Chippewa

Nicolet Nat'l Forest

Marinette
Peshtigo

Lake Wissota

Wisconsin River

Green Bay

Green Bay
Door Peninsula

94

Pentenwell Lake

Lake Poygan

43

La Crosse

Castle Rock Lake

Lake Winnebago

Lake Michigan

Mississippi River

90

Lake Wisconsin

Milwaukee

Madison

94

90

43

Where's My Mooother?

Wisconsin is known as America's Dairyland for its huge herds of dairy cattle that make the state the leading milk producer. These calves have lost their mothers. Draw a line from each cow to her matching calf.

MAP ✔

What's the name of the biggest lake in the state?

-FOR- REAL! On October 8, 1871, the same night as the Chicago fire, the Peshtigo forest fire killed 1,200 people in northeast Wisconsin.

Wyoming

Equality State

Western Meadowlark

Indian Paintbrush

It's a Gusher!

Yellowstone Park is the oldest and biggest national park in the U.S. One of its many attractions is an enormous geyser that spouts steam and water hundreds of feet into the air. Letters that spell the name of this geyser are hidden in this picture. Find the letters and write the geyser's name.

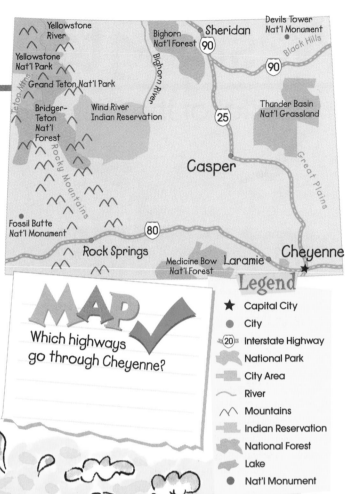

MAP ✓

Which highways go through Cheyenne?

Legend

★ Capital City
● City
⟨20⟩ Interstate Highway
National Park
City Area
River
Mountains
Indian Reservation
National Forest
Lake
● Nat'l Monument

-FOR- REAL!
Wyoming has the fewest people of any state.

Washington, D.C.

The Capital of the United States

Wood Thrush

American Beauty Rose

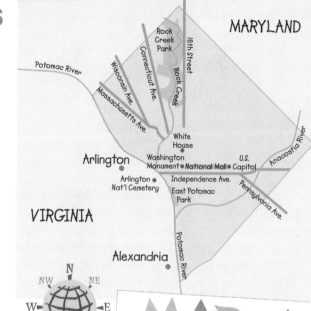

Sight for Sore Eyes

Here are some of the sights visitors see in Washington, D.C. How many can you identify? Write the letters in the boxes.

a. United States Capitol
b. Supreme Court Building
c. Vietnam Veterans Memorial
d. Air and Space Museum
e. White House
f. Jefferson Memorial
g. Lincoln Memorial
h. Original Smithsonian Institution
i. Reflecting Pool

MAP ✓

Which river borders Washington, D.C.?

FOR REAL!

Washington, D.C., is the only U.S. city that is not part of a state. **D.C.** stands for District of Columbia.

Puerto Rico

Commonwealth of the United States

Atlantic Ocean

Arecibo · San Juan ★
Bayamón · Carolina
Sierra del Luquillo
Mayagüez · Cordillera Central
Caguas · Humacao
Sierra de Cayey
Ponce ·
Caribbean Sea

Culebra
El Yunque
Vieques Island

0 10 20 30
miles

A-Mazing Harvest

Circle fruits and other crops as you climb down El Yunque Mountain. How many can you identify?

Legend

★ Capital City
● City
▨▨▨ Expressway
▨ Park
▨ City Area
∼ River
∧∧ Mountains
● Nat'l Monument

MAP ✔

How many miles long is Puerto Rico?

-FOR- REAL! Puerto Ricans are American citizens, but they can't vote and don't pay federal income taxes when they live on the island.

Canada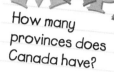

U.S. Neighbor to the North

Maple Leaf Puzzle

The maple leaf is a symbol of Canada. Use the clues to solve the puzzle.

ALBERTA   MONTREAL   LUMBER
ATLANTIC   ENGLISH   EAST
LARGEST   FOOD   PRINCE EDWARD

1. a big city in Quebec

2. a province

3. This island is an eastern province.

4. a forest product of Canada

5. one of Canada's official languages

6. Canada has the __ area of any country in North America.

7. Ontario is __ of Alberta.

8. the ocean that borders Canada on the east

9. In the Prairie Provinces, __ products are important.

Yukon Territory
Northwest Territories
Nunavut
Rocky Mountains
Pacific Ocean
British Columbia
Alberta
Edmonton
Vancouver
Calgary
Saskatchewan
Manitoba
Winnipeg
Hudson Bay
Ontario
Quebec
Newfoundland
Prince Edward Island
Gulf of St Lawrence
Quebec
Montreal
Ottawa
Toronto
New Brunswick
Nova Scotia
Atlantic Ocean

1. M _ _ _ _ _ _ _

2. A _ _ _ _ _ _

3. P _ _ _ _ _ _ _ _ _ _ _

4. L _ _ _ _ _

5. E _ _ _ _ _ _

6. L _ _ _ _ _ _

7. E _ _ _

8. A _ _ _ _ _ _ _

9. F _ _ _

 -FOR- REAL! Canada is the largest country in North America.

Mexico

U.S. Neighbor to the South

MAP ✓
Is the capital of Mexico closer to the northern or southern border?

Viva Mexico!

Play a memory game. Look at these symbols of Mexico for about 30 seconds. Then close the book and see how many you can remember. Compete with a friend if you like.

Mexicali ★

Baja California Norte

Sonora

Hermosillo ★

Gulf of California

Chihuahua ★

Coahuila

Rio Grande

Baja California Sur

Sierra Madre Occidental

Sinaloa

La Paz ★

Culiacán ⊛

Durango ⊛

Saltillo ★

Sierra Madre Oriental

Nuevo León

Monterrey ★

Tamaulipas

Zacatecas ⊛

Ciudad Victoria ★

Aguascalientes ⊛

San Luis Potosí ⊛

Nayarit

Tepic ★

Guanajuato ⊛

Querétaro ⊛

Hidalgo

Pachuca ⊛

Gulf of Mexico

Mérida ★
Yucatán

Guadalajara ⊛

Morelia ⊛

Federal District

Mexico City ★

Jalapa ★

Campeche ★

Quintana Roo

Colima ⊛

Michoacan

Toluca ⊛

México

Tlaxcala ⊛

Veracruz

Tabasco

Chetumal ★

Chilpancingo ★

Puebla ⊛

Villahermosa ★

Pacific Ocean

Guerrero

Sierra Madre Del Sur

Oaxaca ⊛

Tuxtla Gutiérrez ★

Chiapas

Legend
- ★ Capital City
- ⊛ Capital/State Same Name
- ★ National Capital
- ⌃⌃ Mountains

0 100 200 300 400
miles

FOR REAL!

Mexico City has more people than any other city in the world!

The United States

State Abbreviations

Alabama	AL
Alaska	AK
Arizona	AZ
Arkansas	AR
California	CA
Colorado	CO
Connecticut	CT
Delaware	DE
Florida	FL
Georgia	GA
Hawaii	HI
Idaho	ID
Illinois	IL
Indiana	IN
Iowa	IA
Kansas	KS
Kentucky	KY
Louisiana	LA
Maine	ME
Maryland	MD
Massachusetts	MA
Michigan	MI
Minnesota	MN
Mississippi	MS
Missouri	MO
Montana	MT
Nebraska	NE
Nevada	NV
New Hampshire	NH
New Jersey	NJ
New Mexico	NM
New York	NY
North Carolina	NC
North Dakota	ND
Ohio	OH
Oklahoma	OK
Oregon	OR
Pennsylvania	PA
Rhode Island	RI
South Carolina	SC
South Dakota	SD
Tennessee	TN
Texas	TX
Utah	UT
Vermont	VT
Virginia	VA
Washington	WA
West Virginia	WV
Wisconsin	WI
Wyoming	WY

Canada

Atlantic Ocean

N
nw   ne
W   E
sw   se
S

0   200   400   600
miles

Gulf of Mexico

Atlantic Ocean

0 10 20 30 40 50
miles

Puerto Rico

Caribbean Sea

Answers

Page 3 200 miles

Page 4

 north

Page 7

 Mississippi

35 diamonds (including the ace of diamonds)

Page 10

84 = 3", 90 miles,
91 = 2", 60 miles,
95 = 3 1/2", 105 miles

Page 5

 Barrow

xxixxyxnxxyxxlxxx

zzaxxynxxdywyzzz

xaxytxzzyexzrzz

inland water

Page 8

 San Francisco and Sacramento

Page 11

 widest: about 35 miles, narrowest: about 10 miles

29 chickens

Page 6

 40

```
A K S A K B C R O
C B S A G U A R O
P E O S A T N T K
I A N B L T Y Y D
N R P I C E O L E
N C K E S A N L E
A Y H C V I T O R A
C R P O A M E S A
L M Y N L T R U P
E P E L L L R K M
Y C L S E Y A S L
C I K N Y U C C A
H S P B K I E L H
B A N T E L O P E
```

Page 9

 Fort Collins, Greeley, Boulder, Colorado Springs

Page 12

 No; Because the names of some other cities are printed in larger type.

```
B A J H E K B A D A
S W G M Y R T L E S
M I A F D I F W E C
A L L I G A T O R S
N L G S P E L N R A
G O B H E N Z C H W
R W F A L K R C M G
O S U N I B A Y S R
V A G Y C T T P K A
E D H W A H N R B S
S N P A N T H E R S
D Y K I S B A S N Y
H L S N A K E S R A
```

Page 13

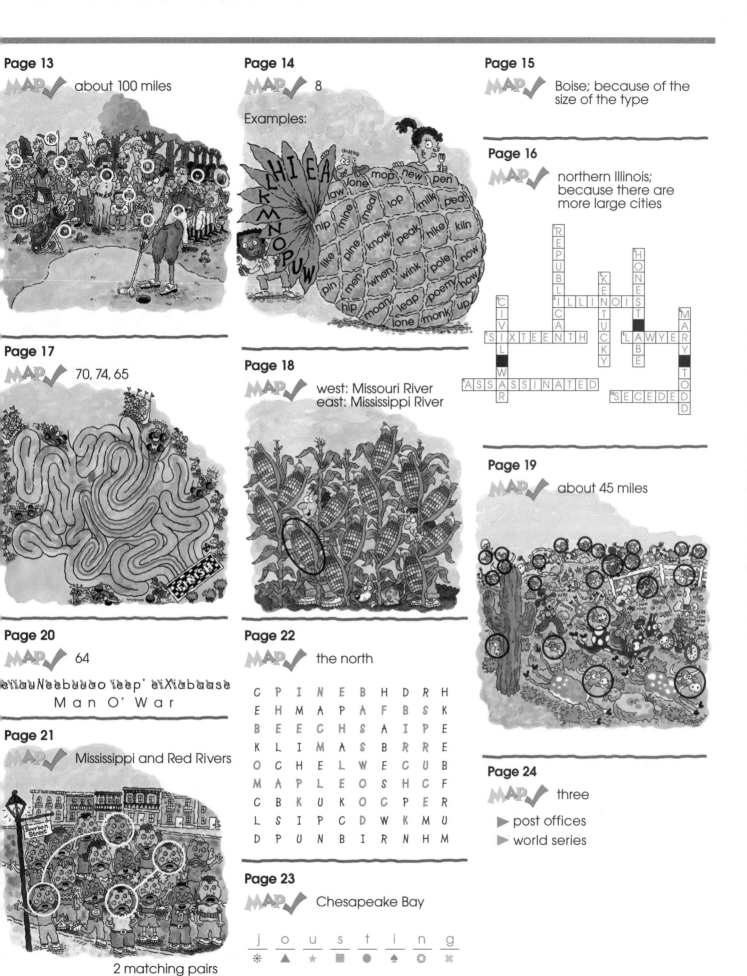

MAP ✓ about 100 miles

Page 14

MAP ✓ 8

Examples:

Page 15

MAP ✓ Boise; because of the size of the type

Page 16

MAP ✓ northern Illinois; because there are more large cities

Crossword:
REPUBLICAN
ILLINOIS
KENTUCKY
HONEST ABE
CIVIL WAR
SIXTEENTH
LAWYER
MARY TODD
ASSASSINATED
SECEDED

Page 17

MAP ✓ 70, 74, 65

Page 18

MAP ✓ west: Missouri River
east: Mississippi River

Page 19

MAP ✓ about 45 miles

Page 20

MAP ✓ 64

Man O' War

Page 21

MAP ✓ Mississippi and Red Rivers

2 matching pairs

Page 22

MAP ✓ the north

```
C  P  I  N  E  B  H  D  R  H
E  H  M  A  P  A  F  B  S  K
B  E  E  C  H  S  A  I  P  E
K  L  I  M  A  S  B  R  R  E
O  C  H  E  L  W  E  C  U  B
M  A  P  L  E  O  S  H  C  F
C  B  K  U  K  O  C  P  E  R
L  S  I  P  C  D  W  K  M  U
D  P  U  N  B  I  R  N  H  M
```

Page 23

MAP ✓ Chesapeake Bay

j o u s t i n g
✳ ▲ ★ ■ ● ♠ ✿ ✖

Page 24

MAP ✓ three

▶ post offices
▶ world series

Page 25

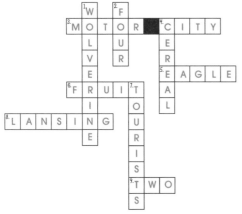 Lakes Michigan, Erie, Huron, and Superior

Across: 3. MOTOR 4. CITY 5. EAGLE 6. FRUIT 8. LANSING 9. TWO
Down: 1. WOLVERINE 2. FUR 4. CEREAL 7. TOURISTS

Page 26

 Superior National Forest; about 150 miles long

Page 29

 seven

Page 32

 Merrimack River

ALAN B. SHEPARD, JR.

Page 30

the east side

```
C O Y O T E S H U P
C S D U C K S R N I
O L O P C B A C L K
T R A E H U P E H E
T A N R O I S D A S
O B R C K E O A C G
N B A H E S O R K P
W I C G C M P S B H
O T C U H B O U E E
O S O D E I P T R A
D R O O R E P L R S
S N N W R S I Y I A
Y M S P I N E S E N
B A D G E R S O S T
N K Y O S K U N K S
```

Page 33

southwest

```
C P U M P K I N S H W P A
A O C R A N B E R R I E S
B T S S G S Q U A S H A N
B A E K R P B I L N P C A
A T O M A T O E S B K H P
G O T E P L E T T U C E B
E E S W E E T C O R N S E
S S Q F S N U L W E A N A
B L U E B E R R I E S P N
S W E E T P O T A T O E S
```

Page 27

about 20 miles

g r o e a p t w i a t f e r
great water

Page 28

 Kansas City

Page 31

Nellis Air Force Range; south

1. LAKE MEAD   2. CACTUS
3. SILVER   4. LAS VEGAS
5. HOOVER DAM 6. FORESTS
7. RENO   8. MINES

RAINFALL

Page 34

 Interstate 25

PUEBLOS

Page 35

 Lakes Erie and Ontario

STATUE OF LIBERTY

Possible words include:

blue	state	latter	tease	yeast
beast	forest	tray	beater	treat

Page 38

 Youngstown

Warren G. Harding—P

Neil A. Armstrong—A

William McKinley—P

William Howard Taft—P

Ulysses S. Grant—P

John H. Glenn, Jr.—A

Orville Wright—I

Thomas A. Edison—I

James A. Garfield—P

Rutherford B. Hayes—P

Wilbur Wright—I

Benjamin Harrison—P

Page 42

 five

53 eggs

Page 36

 no

Page 39

 about 150 miles

Page 43

 triangle

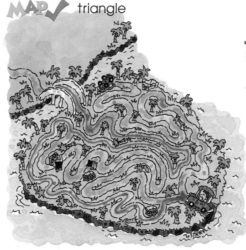

Page 44

 four; Rosebud

George Washington, Thomas Jefferson, Theodore Roosevelt, and Abraham Lincoln

Page 37

MAP ✔ three

T	X	X	X	X	X
X	H	X	X	E	X
X	X	X	B	X	X
A	X	D	X	X	L
X	A	X	X	N	X
X	X	D	X	S	X

THE BADLANDS

Page 40

MAP ✔ Interstate 5

Page 41

MAP ✔ Yes. Philadelphia is bigger.

Page 45

MAP ✔ Great Smoky Mountains, Cumberland Mountains

V	T	E	L	K	N	A	S
H	E	N	T	E	H	P	O
I	N	O	D	N	O	R	U
S	N	R	S	T	V	E	T
A	E	T	U	U	I	R	H
K	S	H	K	C	R	T	C
C	S	C	E	K	G	E	A
G	E	A	T	Y	I	P	R
O	E	R	N	D	N	U	O
H	H	O	Y	O	I	R	L
N	A	L	R	T	A	T	I
I	T	I	N	G	E	L	N
L	V	N	C	K	I	O	A
A	L	A	B	A	M	A	Y

Page 46

MAP ✓ about 770 miles

Crossword:
- 1. ALAMO
- 2. OIL
- 3. MEXICO
- 4. ONE
- 5. AUSTIN
- 6. COWBOY
- 7. SECOND
- 8. BLUE
- 9. CATTLE
- 10. HOUSTON

Page 47

MAP ✓ Interstate 80

Page 50

MAP ✓ about 260 miles

APPLES

CHERRIES

Page 54

MAP ✓ Potomac River

Page 49

MAP ✓ the east part

Page 53

MAP ✓ Interstates 80 and 25

OLD FAITHFUL

Page 55

MAP ✓ about 135 miles

sugar cane
grapefruit
bananas
oranges
pineapple
avocados
coffee

Page 48

MAP ✓ the west side

Page 51

MAP ✓ east: Harpers Ferry
west: Huntington

Page 52

MAP ✓ Lake Winnebago

Page 56

MAP ✓ 10 provinces, 3 territories

1. MONTREAL
2. ALBERTA
3. PRINCE EDWARD
4. LUMBER
5. ENGLISH
6. LARGEST
7. EAST
8. ATLANTIC
9. FOOD

Page 57

MAP ✓ the southern border

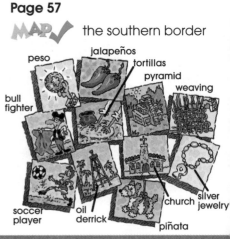

peso
jalapeños
tortillas
pyramid
weaving
bull fighter
oranges
church
silver jewelry
soccer player
oil derrick
piñata